With Faith and Persistence

Living, Learning, Caring

Anthony Meryl Grasse, MD and
Gladys Landis Grasse, RN, BS
with Jean Kilheffer Hess

©2020 Gladys Grasse and StoryShare, LLC

Except where noted otherwise, images from Grasse private collection.

Front cover, historic dish significance: Gladys Landis Grasse purchased the historic dish from J. Walton Angstadt (1915–2016) at a Landis family reunion auction. He collected antiques but none of his children were interested. Walton was the eldest son of Raymond and Annie (Landis) Angstadt; Annie was a sister to Gladys' father, Ephraim Moyer Landis.

The dish symbolizes the connection that linked Gladys and Meryl's families through four generations. It originally belonged to George Rosenberger Landis (1828–1910), great-grandfather of Anthony Meryl Grasse on his maternal side (Lillian Landis Grasse). George's brother was Ephraim Rosenberger Landis (1824–1901), great-grandfather of Gladys Landis Grasse.

Back cover: A. Meryl and John L. Grasse families in front of the original clinic on Highway 56, Calico Rock, Arkansas, circa 1963. Back Row: Meryl, Gladys, Mary Margaret, and John L.; Front Row: Carol, Chloe, Karen, Nancy, Mark, Philip (rear), Gwendolyn, and Joel.

Cover and interior design by Beth Oberholtzer
Cover Photo by MrFabPhotos, Phillip Michael Whitley

ISBN 978-0-9832977-9-6

Dedication & Acknowledgements

This book of our life stories is dedicated to the many people who have been involved in the medical work in Arkansas. John L. and Mary Margaret Grasse (Meryl's brother and brother's wife) moved to Calico Rock, Arkansas, in 1952 soon after we arrived and helped to set up laboratory and x-ray in the clinic and later in the hospital, provided nursing care (Mary Margaret) and served as hospital administrator (John L.); Mennonite volunteers from Pennsylvania helped build the 10-bed hospital with outpatient clinic in 1958; Mennonite nurses moved to Arkansas from outside locations to work in the hospital; Dr. John M. and Betty Grasse (Meryl and John L. Grasse's first cousin and wife) maintained the clinic and hospital while Meryl and Gladys went to work in Nigeria from 1964 to 1967 and stayed on until 1970; Lewis Bell, Calico Rock, Arkansas, supervised the hospital construction and numerous additions with the help of many local workers. Many dedicated local residents of Calico Rock, Arkansas, and surrounding area work as staff and physicians in the clinic and hospital, serve on the hospital board of trustees and hospital auxiliary, and today maintain the "Community Medical Center of Izard County."

—A. Meryl Grasse and Gladys Landis Grasse

Crepe myrtles in bloom at the Mennonite cemetery in Calico Rock, Arkansas

Contents

Gladys' Story — 1
Grandparents — 1
Uncle Howard — 3
A Home for Reuben — 4
Growing Up in Blooming Glen, Pennsylvania — 5
Elementary through High School Days — 10
Faith and Church — 13
Anthony Grasse Military Service — 15
Nursing School and College — 16
Getting to Know Meryl, Getting to Know Arkansas — 20
Setting up a Medical Practice — 25
Parenting — 28
A Hospital is Born — 30
Nigeria Experience — 38
Mennonite Church in Calico Rock — 44
Our Parents' Later Years — 45
Homes we Built — 47

Meryl's Story — 49
Grasse Family Name — 49
Grandparents — 49
Valued: Education & Religion — 50
Farm Life and Food — 53
Father's War Stories — 53

Huckster's Helper	54
Elementary and Secondary Schooling	55
Goshen College	59
Hahnemann Medical School	64
Overseas Service, Then Marriage	67
Medical Practice, Calico Rock, Arkansas	69
Nigeria Adventure	73
Our Land	76

Country Doctor Stories — 77

Barter for Medical Care	77
Bertha's Story	77
When is She Going to Die?	78
Kid with a Painful Stomach	78
"We Didn't Send a Whole Lot Out"	78
Ferryman's Cyst	79
Reminiscing	79
House Call: Faith and Medicine	80
Sharing Food in Appreciation for Medical Care	80
Letter to the Editor	81
Queen Elizabeth Roses	81
Treated in Such a Special Way	82

Tidbits and Timelines — 83

Family Recipes: Culinary Tastings Across Cultures — 97

Gallery — 109

Genealogy — 127

Gladys' Forebears	127
Meryl's Forebears	127
Gladys & Meryl Descendants	128

Introduction

Meryl and Gladys Grasse grew up within three miles of each other in Bucks County, Pennsylvania—Meryl on a farm in the Hilltown area and Gladys in the village of Blooming Glen. When they married in 1952, they set off on an adventure to live in the rural, mountainous Ozarks of Arkansas to provide medical care. They had no idea they would build a hospital, raise six children, and live in Nigeria for a short stint over the coming years. They claimed Arkansas as their home for 63 years.

In North American Mennonite history, America's world wars were crucial turning points. At the onset of WWII (1939–1945), President Roosevelt created Civilian Public Service (CPS) to provide members of historic peace churches an alternative to military service. Forestry and agricultural services as well as healthcare figured prominently in the options offered. These activities took Mennonite young people out of their ethnic and religious communities into the larger world, which stimulated social awareness and a new sense of social responsibility.[1]

In the late 1940s, Dr. Meryl Grasse was invited to visit Culp, Arkansas, where they were searching for a doctor. The Mennonite Board of Missions had started rural mission work in Culp in 1935, set up a school, a clinic, and several churches to serve an isolated community where there were almost no resources for education or healthcare.

These are the stories of Meryl and Gladys (Landis) Grasse as they remember their lives and personal histories, a mosaic of oral history and written documentation. There may be other versions of some of these stories that have been shared elsewhere. Their stories tell of growing up in Pennsylvania in the Mennonite faith and culture, moving to and settling in the Ozarks in Arkansas, and engaging in international work in various countries.

---

1. **Source**: Mennonites in American Society, 1930–1970: Modernity and the Persistence of Religious Community (Mennonite Experience in America, Vol. 4.) Paul Toews. Scottdale, Pennsylvania: Herald Press, 1999.

Gladys' Story

Gladys Stover Landis Grasse (b. January 17, 1926)

Grandparents

My mother's parents were Ida Baum and Edwin Stover. When Mother was a sophomore in high school, her mother died of a diabetic coma during the night. She had diabetes, but at that time they didn't have insulin. Her death was rather sudden.

After my grandmother passed away, my grandfather wanted Mother to quit school in the second year of high school. Mother didn't want to quit school—she loved school! She was great at math and participated in math competitions. But because her younger brother, Willard, was at home yet, her dad wanted her to stay home and help take care of the house. So she left school.

Gladys' maternal grandmother Ida Baum Stover.

Gladys' mother, Mamie Stover, as a girl.

Gladys' maternal grandfather, Ed Stover, at two different stages of life.

My grandfather Ed Stover had a feed mill in Blooming Glen, Pennsylvania, the only feed mill there. Besides taking care of the home my mother also worked in the office at the mill doing bookkeeping and things like that.

So I knew Ed Stover, but he died when I was two. They tell me that he was a bank director and he would take me along to the bank sometimes. In my mind I visualize riding with him in the car to the bank: I don't know if it's from the stories they tell me or if it's a real memory.

My grandfather married again and had a second wife, Vena Weaver Martin. I remember her more, my step-grandmother. As a young child I lived next door to them, and I would go over sometimes and eat with them. My mother's side of the family had a hard time dealing with the second wife "replacing their mother." But I always related to them.

After Vena became a widow she lived in another place across the street from the old place. I'd connect with Vena and her daughter Grace Martin. When I was about nine years old, Grace gave me my first book, *Little Women* by Louisa May Alcott, and thus began my interest in reading.

Vena also had a son, Wayne Martin, but my family related more to Grace. I don't know why. My siblings said, "That wasn't right," because they'd invite Grace to family reunions later on, but not the son, Wayne. We could never understand it.

On my Dad's side, my grandparents were Reuben and Lizzie Landis. Lizzie was small and frail, and Reuben was big and heavyset. I might have been about 8 when she died. All I remember of her was going to visit every Sunday at their house on the farm at Dublin, Pennsylvania, and she was already upstairs in bed.

I hear that she died of consumption, so I figure that it was tuberculosis because I have a positive reaction to tuberculosis tests now.

My paternal grandparents lived on one side of the farmhouse, and their daughter and her husband lived on the other side. So when we visited them, the adults would meet on my grandparents' side, and we cousins would all go over on the other side and play Rook and things around the table. We had a high old time! I remember we had enough heavy snows that we could build tunnels on the farm and go through with our sleds.

I never had much of a relationship with my grandfather Reuben, well not with my grandmother Lizzie either because I remember her mostly in bed in her later years. But my grandfather, I always remember—I hate to say this, but—his children didn't have much respect for him. He was always interested in money, and he was a harsh disciplinarian. I grew up not having much respect for him because he was like that.

My father told about one time when one of the children came in from the barn with a basket full of eggs and fell. My grandmother Lizzie, this little, short slim woman, quickly ran out and protected the child from my grandfather. I think they buried the eggs so he wouldn't see they were broken, since she knew he would be pretty harsh with the child.

Reuben and Lizzie had twelve children, and there were two sets of twins. My father was part of one of the sets of twins. In each of the sets, one twin died early. One died at about eight months old, and the other one died in infancy. They called them "the runts."

Uncle Howard

My grandfather made my uncle—Howard, my father's brother—leave the farm. Then he got his daughter, Lizzie, and her husband, Warren, to move in on the other side of the house. Warren was a match for him. He didn't tolerate anything from Reuben.

Uncle Howard bought a farm up the road and moved there. At that time they had "Aid children[2]" that would come in the home and help. I remember Ed Schultz was one of the Aid children there at that time, and my brother's family and I still keep in contact with him. So he had lived with my uncle, and he always feels like a part of the family.

---

2. Aid children—Children's Aid Society of Pennsylvania (CAS of PA) was formed in 1882 and was one of the first organizations dedicated to the care of children who were homeless. Founded for the care and training of neglected and homeless children, they are trained in "self-reliance and habits of industry."

One day in the winter when a heavy snow came, the milk trucks couldn't get in for several weeks. Howard couldn't ship the milk out, so he was losing money. They found him hanging in the barn. We don't know what other kinds of financial challenges he may have been facing on the farm.

One of Howard's girls was my age—I was off at college—and the other girl, Pauline, was my sister's age. When Marian, my sister, came home for lunch from high school, they wanted her to tell Pauline about her father. But Marian said, "I can't do that." So my mother and father told Pauline about her father's death. It was a hard thing in the family.

My Dad always regretted that he didn't know more about his brother's finances. He said, "I would have helped him if I'd have known." He always felt guilty. At that time the Mennonite Church would not allow anybody who committed suicide to have a funeral in the church, so that was hard on the family.

A Home for Reuben

When my grandmother, Lizzie, died, my grandfather Reuben wanted to live with one of the children. Well, they didn't know what to do because none of them wanted him full-time! The children decided he could move around every six months and stay with different ones.

Our family home wasn't that big, and Mother was trying to decide how we were going to keep Reuben for six months. We had just three bedrooms. My twin brothers were in one, my sister and I in the

Above left: Gladys' paternal grandparents Reuben and Lizzie Moyer Landis. Above: Farm of Gladys' paternal grandparents Reuben and Lizzie Moyer Landis in Dublin, Pennsylvania.

other, and my parents in the third bedroom. I think they were planning to get a sofa bed in our home for Reuben or for some of us children to use.

When his children told him the plan for moving every six months, he said, "I'm not going to do that! I'm going to go to the nursing home." So he went to the nursing home, and that problem was solved.

At the nursing home he met a woman whom he married, Julia, who was not as submissive to him. She wasn't like his first wife. He met his match.

Growing Up in Blooming Glen, Pennsylvania

My mother, Mamie Stover, met my dad, Ephraim Landis, at the Stover Feed Mill in Blooming Glen, Pennsylvania, which was owned by her father. She worked at the feed mill and Eph would come in and buy feed. After they married, they lived in a house right next to my Stover grandparents.

There were three sisters in my mother's family, Mamie, Maria (pronounced Moriah) and Katie Stover. The sisters never moved off of the same street in Blooming Glen. Their husbands got jobs in the Stover Feed Mill, which they ran, along with the sisters' two brothers Arthur and Willard. Later on they also started a mill in Perkasie, Pennsylvania.

Before my sister was born and when I was about five, we moved up the street to another house on the same block. Our address was 136 E. State Street. That's where I grew up. Then my Aunt Katie and Uncle Ervin Moyer moved into my Stover grandparents' home after Ed Stover died. Aunt Maria and Uncle Frank lived midway between the two other families.

Mamie Stover and Ephraim Landis, Gladys' parents, as young people.

Stover sisters who loved each other's company so much they lived on the same street in Blooming Glen throughout their lives. Left to right, 1977: Katie Moyer, Maria Alderfer, and Mamie Landis.

With Faith and Persistence

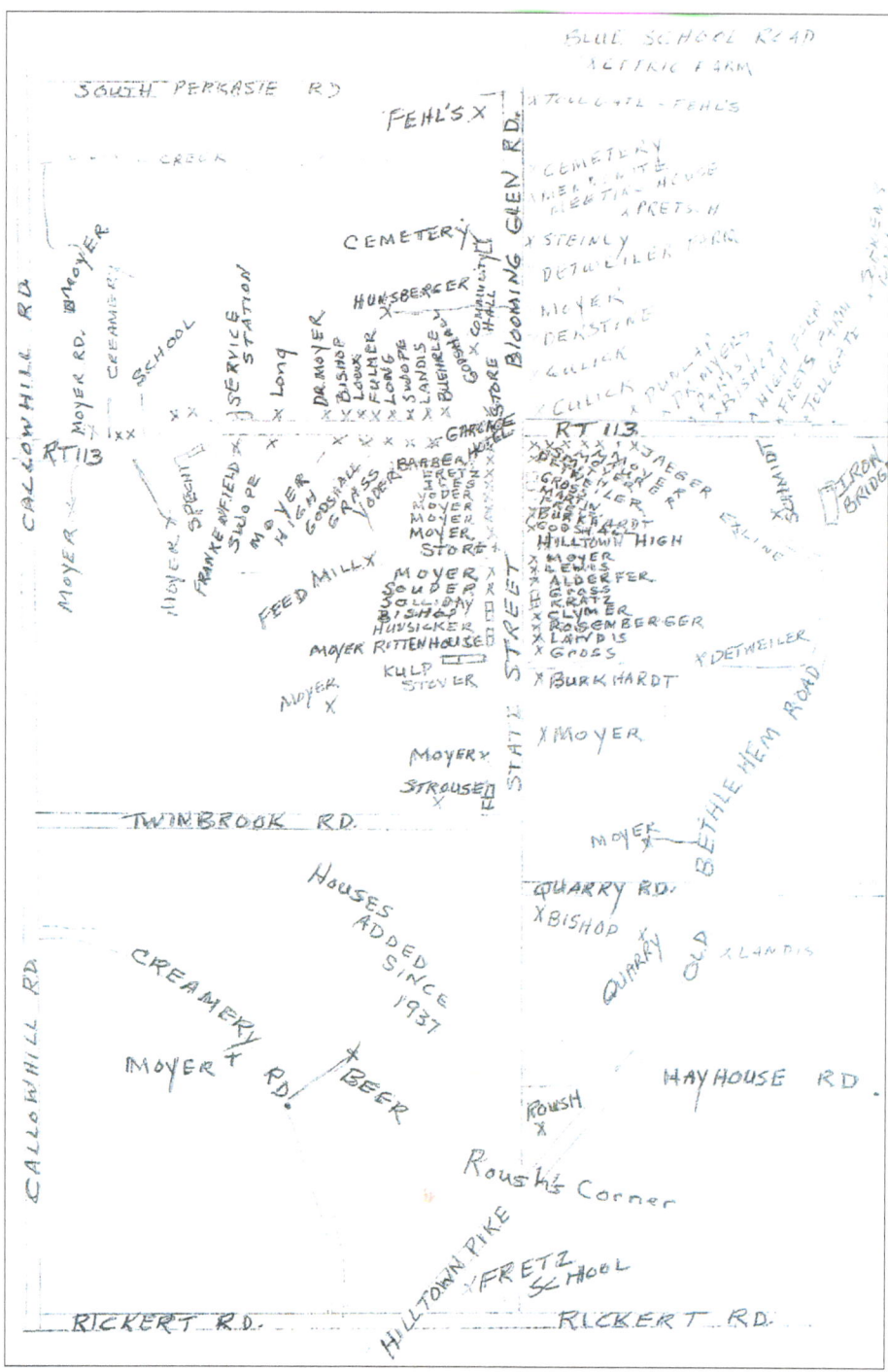

Hand Drawn map of Blooming Glen, Pennsylvania from Blooming Glen—Remembered *by Edna Mae Lewis Loux, self published, 2010. Gladys' house on right side of the street by the R in State Street; Aunt Maria and Frank Alderfer lived five houses up on same side of street; Aunt Katie and Erv Moyer lived on other side of the street just below "Yoder;" Bishop's store is at the corner of Rt. 113 and State St.; Shaddinger's Store is across the street and up a few houses from Gladys' house. Shaddinger's Store also had the town post office in it.*

Aerial shot of Blooming Glen with Stover's Feed Mill in the foreground.

Gladys as a baby and as a young child.

Above: Gladys on the porch of the house in which she grew up. Right: Gladys' family of origin, left to right: Mamie Stover Landis holding Ray Landis, Marian Landis, Gladys Landis, Ephraim Landis holding Roy Landis.

Gladys and her siblings circa 1952. Left to right: Roy Landis, Gladys Landis, Marian Landis, Ray Landis.

My twin brothers, Ray and Roy, were born in May 1938 when I was 12 years old. Marian, my sister, and I were born at home, but they were born at Grandview Hospital. On the day they were born, my cousin Ruth Alderfer and I went around town knocking on doors telling everyone the news of their birth. They had to stay several weeks in the hospital since they were barely four pounds at birth. My mother would pump breast milk, and then at noon Dad would come home from work and take me to the hospital to deliver the milk. I guess he didn't want to go into the hospital in his work clothes.

Dad would have loved to have a farm. Sunday afternoons we'd drive around and see these farms that he liked. We almost moved one time because he found a farm in Hilltown, Pennsylvania, but Mother could never leave Blooming Glen and that street with her sisters. That was something. We always laughed about that: they never moved off the same street.

During the time I was at college the feed mill in Blooming Glen burned one night. They don't know what started it, but the neighbors said they saw a car pull out of there that night. My parents lived just up the street from the mill, and Dad ran and got one truck out yet. One side of his face and his arms were red from the heat. That was hard on the family to lose that mill. So then they all went up

Above: Stover's Feed Mill employees, left to right: H. Yoder, Ephraim Landis (Gladys' father), J. Swope, C. Stover, O. Kratz, F. Alderfer (Aunt Maria's husband), E. Moyer (Aunt Katie's husband). Above right: Stover's Feed Mill, Blooming Glen, Pennsylvania. Right: Feed truck loaded for delivery.

to the Stover Feed Mill at Perkasie, a town about six miles away, and worked there.

My father just had an eighth grade education, but he became a bank director later on.[3] I always wondered how that came about. I know he had a good friend on the bank board that told him to come in and be a bank director. He must have had good financial knowledge.

As a child I had to help around the house. I always hated cleaning. My sister was more the cleaner. Also Dad had chickens, and we had eggs that we would sell. I remember sitting on the cellar steps cleaning eggs. That was a job. I remember the crates that we'd put the eggs in after we cleaned them. I don't know if he sold them to "hucksters"[4] or what. Now I've learned that if you want to have fresher eggs you don't clean them until you're ready to use them.

I remember my parents having dandelion wine down in the cellar too. And that was good! It was for colds. It sort of put you to sleep. I know how it warmed you. As I grew older they decided it wasn't good to have it down there anymore.

Blooming Glen was a nice little village to grow up in. It was sort of a Mennonite village, but then interspersed there were some who attended the Reformed Church. And I remember when an Italian family moved in. The next door neighbors on the one side of our house were Reformed, and they had two girls and a boy. The girls, Elsie and Stella, were important in my life.

---

3. He was a director of Peoples Bank. It later merged with Univest Bank.
4. A huckster is a seller of produce and farm products.

With Faith and Persistence

Next door neighbor, mentor, and friend, Stella (left) and Gladys standing by Stella's house, about 1930.

Right across the street, there were girls my age. Next door were the Burkharts—they weren't a Mennonite family, but they had a boy and two girls. We all mingled together on that street.

I remember when we got roller skates. We'd roller skate down the walk. And we'd go all the way down to Rt. 113 on those roller skates and do things like that together. I mean, it couldn't have been a better village.

The Hilltown High School, where I went, was just about six or eight houses down the street. It was a three-year high school, so we had to go somewhere else for our senior year. My parents decided it would be better if I'd transfer my junior year to learn to make friends and have them two years. So I went to Souderton High School which was about ten miles away. I rode to school with my neighbor, Elsie, who worked at Harleysville Insurance, and she picked me up after school. I had to wait at school and do some studying until she came along.

Elsie's sister Stella became a nurse. When she came home weekends from her nursing studies at Grand View Hospital, the local nursing school, I'd go over and talk to her about being a nurse. I always wanted to be a nurse from little on up, and this influenced me all the more.

The celebrities and Broadway shows were coming out of New York City and performing in tents at New Hope, Pennsylvania, a town beyond Doylestown. When I was about 14, Elsie and Stella were going over there to one of these shows, and they asked my parents if I could go along. Well, Mennonites at that time didn't go to movies or anything, and I thought, "Oh, they're not gonna let me." But they thought it over, and they left me go. I thought, "Boy, now I'm an adult! This is great getting out in the world!" Elsie and Stella had a lot of influence on me.

Elementary Through High School Days

In Blooming Glen Elementary School, we had Mrs. Solliday. She was a good teacher, very good for the elementary grades. It was a two-room school with two stories. On the first floor were the first four grades, and Mrs. Solliday taught those. On the second were fourth to eighth grade, and we had a man teacher, Poppy Yoder, and he was good.

It was a township school, and there were one-room schools all around the township. We'd come together once a year, all those schools, and have a program at the Community Hall in Blooming Glen. That was a big day. Each school had to give a program. It was just a sort of a community thing.

Some of the women teachers at some of the other one-room schools got these boys as students who came out of the city and were living in Hilltown in what we would call foster care today. These teachers were more meek and mild and couldn't discipline these big burly guys, so they'd send them off to Poppy's school. Anyone that had a problem in one of the other schools in the district would send them to Poppy Yoder.

We had double seats, you know, two desks together. Poppy brought those guys in, and if they got out of control he took them out of that seat and gave them a good shaking. But then he'd go out on the ball field and play with them as if nothing had ever happened. The one who sat in the seat next to that guy got out when they knew that Poppy was coming to discipline them.

I always respected Poppy. When I was his student, sometimes some of those guys who had gotten out of school would come back after graduation, and they'd say, "I remember that seat. You did me some good there." But today that kind of discipline would be considered abusive, and that teacher would be fired. Those were the days when the parents backed up the teachers.

I remember in the elementary school the ones that were ahead in the other grades would help the others that were a little behind in first grade. And that was good. Now teachers usually have an assistant. Mrs. Solliday didn't have anybody to assist her; it was the students who assisted.

Blooming Glen Community Hall where each school gave its annual program.

Blooming Glen Grade School.

And those that were ahead of their lessons in first grade, they'd hear her teaching other grades, and they gained knowledge and weren't bored then in their class. It was a good education.

We did a lot of memory work in fourth through eighth grades. I remember we had to stand up front and memorize poems and things like the Gettysburg Address.

The school was outside of town, and we all walked to school about half to three-quarters of a mile. In the morning we would start out, and as you walked down more kids came out, and you were all walking together.

There were two stores in town. One was Shaddinger's General Store which had a post office in it and was on the street across from the Hilltown High School. When you got down around the corner, there was Bishop's Store. My mother often sent along a penny or two so we could stop at Bishop's and get something for recess, a little snack like candy, and take that along to school.

Aerial view of Blooming Glen, looking east on Route 113.

Bishop's Store where Gladys often stopped to buy candy on the way to school.

Hilltown High School.

Then coming home, it was just a crowd of us walking home from school. And those were our friends. We had a good time! We didn't have to worry about somebody picking somebody up—it was a very safe environment.

When I got to Hilltown High School, John M. Grasse, Meryl's uncle, was our principal. There were two courses of study in high school: the Academic Course or the Business Course. I wanted to be a nurse, and to be a nurse you had to take the Academic Course.

At Souderton, during my last two years of high school, I always wanted to take typing. But I could never work it in because I had to take Latin as part of the Academic Course, and that sort of upset me. Now I don't know how to type, and with this computer age,[5] I just pick one key at a time. I always blame the schools for that, because I wanted to take typing and saw how important it was. And look

---

5. Gladys bought an iPad at age 82 and moved into the computer age.

how we've lost Latin along the way. You don't need it for nurse's training anymore either.

And oh, plane geometry. That teacher taught to the "A" students. We others sort of, you know, we'd just slide through on it. I don't know how I passed geometry.

We had a classmate Russell Rickert. He was from a poor family of fifteen children, but those children were all "A" students. They were knowledgeable. I remember Russell coming to school with his head shaved. His father always cut their hair, and he shaved it so he wouldn't have to cut it as often. My father delivered feed to the Rickert farm, and all 15 children worked on the farm from a young age.

Now I have a book that Russell Rickert wrote, "Life on the Farm," 1985. In the book he says that whenever they wore out shoes, if there was one good shoe, their mother kept it in a closet. When they needed new shoes, they got shoes out of there, and they didn't always match. They'd come to school with two different shoes on. I can't remember if the kids made fun of them or not. Russell became a professor at a college.[6] So it just shows you how families survived at that time, without government welfare.

Faith and Church

Most of the families in Blooming Glen were Mennonite and many attended Blooming Glen Mennonite Church, so the church played a big role in our lives. At that time we'd have revival meetings, and these Mennonite evangelists would come in and speak. The minute they thought it was time for you to join church, the evangelist and the ministers would come around to your house and talk to you.

I was sort of rebellious. I thought, "They shouldn't make me join church." So when they came around I decided I wasn't going to join church. I was about 14, and I refused. I don't know what my parents thought after they left.

But then all my friends were joining. So after all that was over—near baptism time—I decided I'd better go along with the class. But it wasn't sincere. Then when I was about 20, I made a recommitment that was more sincere. Now they don't pressure you to join the church anymore. They let you make your own decision.

At that time we wore coverings (prayer veils worn by Mennonite women.) You had to wear strings on your covering, I think, to be baptized. Also when the conference minister, who was John Lapp at that time, came around to shake

Gladys dressed for Class Day during high school graduation festivities.

---

6. Russell Rickert became dean of the School of Sciences and Mathematics, West Chester University, West Chester, Pennsylvania.

With Faith and Persistence

The Old Mennonite Meetinghouse at Blooming Glen. Dedicated Nov. 26, 1882 and razed June 27, 1938. Gladys remembers attending church here.

hands the Sunday before to approve your taking communion. After the church service you had to go up front and shake hands with him to signal that you were okay to take communion. And you had to wear strings then. We young people all put the strings on for that, but the next day the strings came off.

Many years later, after John Lapp's wife had died, he was travelling around the country with his brother-in-law, and they stopped in at Arkansas and stayed with us for a night. He was a good friend of Lillian Grasse, Meryl's mother, and they stopped in to see her. I remember thinking, "I never thought I'd entertain John Lapp!" and also, "Oh, what a change he has seen in the church!"

I remember that the Mennonite Church, when I was young, chose its leaders 'by lot' yet. My uncle, Frank Alderfer, who was married to my mother's sister, Maria (they lived in the middle section on our street,) came up in the 'lot' for deacon.

To be chosen by lot, several hymnbooks or Bibles equal to the number of candidates were placed on a table, and each held a slip of paper. One slip had words or a verse written on it. A prayer for divine action was offered, and each candidate took one of the books and opened it. The one who found the lot slip was determined as the one God had chosen.

Frank and Maria's daughter, Ruth, was one year younger than me, and we were good friends. I remember that day at the church. They had the service. And the way it worked then was that immediately after the service, the church ministers and leaders went to the home of the one who was chosen by lot and had a meal with them. So the wives had to be ready for a meal in case their

14

husbands were chosen. Also, Uncle Frank had to wear a "plain"[7] coat and Aunt Maria had to wear "cape"[8] dresses. She had some nice dresses she could not wear anymore. I wish I'd have asked Mother more questions about these things when she was living.

Ruth and I were walking home from church, and as we got up near Shaddinger's Store, we looked across the street, and all these cars were around their house. "Uh oh, her dad got picked by lot." It was hard on him.

I didn't realize how hard until my brother Ray reminded me recently that the deacon always read the Scripture at the church service and then had a prayer afterward. Uncle Frank had a hard time praying publicly at first, Ray said, and often times he would say, after the Scripture, "And now we will kneel for silent prayer." That was when you kneeled at your benches, on your knees. Later, he became more comfortable praying publicly.

But Aunt Maria was very faithful. She went with Frank on visitation and served good meals when they had company. My Aunt Katie had moved into Edwin Stover's house (my grandfather), and they just had one son. They had a room upstairs, so when any evangelist came to church, they stayed at her house in that upper room. Then they had their quiet time to prepare their sermons. They said Aunt Katie had "The Upper Room[9]" at her house.

Anthony Grasse Military Service

In Meryl's family, his father, Anthony Grasse, grew up as a Baptist. He served in the First World War. But afterwards he became a Mennonite and a pacifist when he married Meryl's mother, Lillian Landis Grasse. The Grasse family had a hard time with him marrying a Mennonite and becoming pacifist.

Meryl's dad wouldn't talk to his sons much about the war and being in those trenches and things, but he talked to our children. "War isn't the answer," he

---

7. Plain coat—In Colonial America the man's coat was a frock coat without lapel, buttoned to the throat. In the 19th Century, Mennonite ministers in general objected to changes as the collar rose higher and turned over to form the modern roll collar. Mennonite deviations in dress from the conventions of the surrounding culture are regarded by many as symbols of nonconformity to the world. Source: *Global Anabaptist Mennonite Encyclopedia Online.* http://gameo.org/

8. Cape dress—long dress with a cape or other second layer to cover the bosom. Fabrics are usually solids or simple prints. Distinctive and plain garb has been characteristic of many Mennonites. Source: *Global Anabaptist Mennonite Encyclopedia Online.* http://gameo.org/

9. The Upper Room in the Bible was traditionally held to be the site where Jesus and the disciples met for the Last Supper.

Anthony Grasse and Lillian Landis, circa 1920.

said. "It was horrible." Anthony's grandchildren learned more from him about the war than we did, because by that time he felt the need to talk more about it.

We divided his military uniform clothes among the Grasse children, but later on the Mennonite Heritage Museum in Harleysville, Pennsylvania, wanted the military outfit from someone who became pacifist. So we gathered that all together, and they have it in the museum and display it every once in a while.

Meryl's parents and grandparents lived near the Baptist Church in Hilltown. On Sunday mornings, Meryl's grandmother Bertha Landis, who was Mennonite, would teach at the Blooming Glen Mennonite Church. In the afternoon she'd go across the street from her house and teach at the Baptist Church. They had Sunday school there in the afternoon.

Meryl's dad's brother, John M. Grasse, married Meryl's mother's sister, Blanche Landis, so two brothers married two sisters. Meryl's dad's brother always stayed Baptist, but his wife was Mennonite. She'd go to the Mennonite church, and he'd go to the Baptist church. Their children all became Mennonite. But when she died, he buried her in the Baptist cemetery. We always said to Mother Grasse, "How do you feel about your sister being buried there?" She'd say, "Doesn't matter where you are if you die." It was always interesting how they dealt with the Mennonite and Baptist differences.

Nursing School and College

When I got out of high school I decided to go to nursing school at Grand View Hospital, in Sellersville, Pennsylvania. It was a smaller hospital back then than it is today. There were no intensive care units at that time. We had private rooms, and we had wards.

A ward is a big room with many beds and not much privacy—just curtains between the beds. We had a women's ward and a men's ward. And we had a little tiny space where we put children; it was just a four-bed ward, and that wasn't always filled.

I liked to take care of the children we had there. One child that I took care of, we were going to do tonsillectomy surgery on her and her brothers. But when they did the lab work, they saw in her blood that she had something wrong that she'd bleed easily. It was something they could not correct. So they didn't do the surgery on her.

I think it was a Mennonite family, and I just felt so sorry for them and so hopeless, you know. It really hit me hard that they came in for normal surgery and went out with this diagnosis that they couldn't help her. I think later on the girl died.

As part of our training we were in Philadelphia for nine months getting experience in bigger hospitals, both Children's Hospital and Pennsylvania Hospital, which was the nation's first hospital founded in 1751 by Benjamin Franklin. At Pennsylvania Hospital you could see yet where they had chained mentally ill patients in the basement there.

We'd go back and forth on the train. You'd go down to Lansdale and go on the train to the Reading Terminal in Philadelphia. Then we could all walk down to 8th and Spruce Street to Pennsylvania Hospital. The Children's Hospital was at 8th and Bainbridge. I appreciated that, that we had a time in the city.

Pennsylvania Hospital was L-shaped. One part was a 12-bed ward, and the other was a 20-bed ward. They had the worst cases over in this 12-bed ward, and we had just one student nurse taking care of those 12 beds. When I think of the responsibilities we had in those days, oh man! And we did 12-hour shifts sometimes.

Penicillin came in when I was nursing. That was something. Now when we look at it, it was such weak doses. Now we hardly use penicillin anymore.[10]

I know at Grand View, at night when we did 12-hour shifts, they had a place on the third floor where we could take a nap if we wanted to. They gave us a little time to go up and nap because we had classes the next day!

We had a nursing school teacher who never married, and I remember one time she said, "If you find somebody you really love, and you have the chance, don't turn it down." We figured that at one time she had a chance to get married and didn't and regretted it.

She was very strict on some things. We had to wear hair nets and we never had them down far enough on our foreheads. She'd always tell us to pull them down more. So one day we all came to class with them pulled way down, almost over our eyes! I'm surprised she didn't get upset and discipline us. I don't know what happened, but we took a picture of the class all standing with our hairnets pulled down low.

When we were living and working in Philadelphia, there were some Mennonite medical students down there too. Meryl was one of them; he was studying at Hahnemann Medical School. We'd get together in a sort of Mennonite meeting fellowship with all these different students.

We entered in August, 1943, and we were capped on March 12, 1944. We remember traveling to Abington Hospital three days a week for classes in the sciences; wearing hair nets to our eyebrows; and Gladys Landis' case study being on the Student Page of the DAVIS NURSING SURVEY, May, 1945. On May 21, 1946, we were the first class to have all starting students graduate. Q.A.W. Rohrbach, Ph.D. was the speaker at the ceremony held at the Souderton High School. The annual banquet was held at the Owl's Nest with Dr. P.T. Moyer as speaker. Miss Margaret I. Bowen was president of the Alumnae Association this year.
A communication from the Pennsylvania State Board of Examiners for the Registration of Nurses read "It was interesting to note that out of 123 schools in the state whose graduates wrote the exam in 1946 Grand View was one of four schools in which there were no failures."

The hair net rebellion   Posing

Grandview Nursing School students who took part in the "Hairnet Rebellion, 1943.

---

10. Penicillin was discovered in 1928 by Alexander Fleming in London, England; it was first used in the United States in the early 1940s. Penicillin, the first antibiotic, was a "wonder drug" that treated diseases caused by bacterial infections.

From Grand View Hospital School of Nursing Reflection Book, the Class of 1946. Left to right, back row: Naomi Derstein, Irene Swauger, Dorothy Trauger, Gladys Landis, Jean Wentz, Betty Gross, Gladys Wood. Front row: Marion Clemens, Florence Yothers, Molly Brown, Kathryn Hockman, Betty Ahlum.

Gladys and friends in Old White House Dorm at Grand View Hospital.

Even though we grew up in the same congregation, I hadn't known Meryl at Blooming Glen Church. He was three grades ahead of me, and we had a big enough church to always have your own Sunday School grade. I remembered John, his brother. I knew him better.

When we were both part of the Mennonite student fellowship in Philadelphia, Meryl asked me on a date. He took me to the opera Figaro. When we got to the opera, he said, "Well now this is a true Mennonite date. I couldn't get tickets together, so we have to sit separately. We'll meet at intermission." I thought, "Why didn't he tell me that before? He tells me now when we get here?!"

I think Meryl and I had one other date, we went to another opera. We didn't know each other that well, and neither one of us, I think, were impressed.

After I graduated from nurse's training with a 3-year RN (Registered Nurse) degree, I worked for a year as a nurse at Grand View. A lot of my friends were at college, and I thought, "I'll go out there to Goshen College in Indiana and join them and get a Bachelor of Science degree in nursing."

My dad had paid for my nurse's training—it was something like $300, books and uniform. But when I told him about my interest in college he said, "I paid for your nursing, but I'm not going to pay for college." (Even Meryl's father was not supportive of him going to college.)

Gladys' Story

Left: Gladys graduated from nursing school in 1946.
Gladys and her Plymouth.

I wanted to go to college and get an all-around education, because all we did was talk about medicine in our nursing education. I wanted to learn more about what was out there. Even though my father wasn't going to help me, I decided I'd go on my own, pay my own way, and try and get through myself. I enrolled at Goshen College.

There were about 10 nurses there at Goshen College who had been in a three-year nursing program and were enrolling for B.S. degrees. The college was thinking about starting its own nursing program. I know they were working on it when we were there.

At that time the average student who was going to college and working part-time was earning 45 cents an hour. We nurses would ride the bus to Elkhart Hospital and do private duty nursing—this was before they had intensive care—and we would earn a dollar an hour. We were earning good wages and helping our education.

I really enjoyed taking art. I'm not an art person, but I enjoy learning about art. I enjoyed Shakespeare! I took some electives that weren't for the B.S. and didn't take enough of the core courses, so I had to go to summer school to graduate. I liked that summer school because you concentrated; in a few weeks you took a course. I took Shakespeare, and I just enjoyed it. I was amazed and glad I got that opportunity.

College widened my world. I got to know other people outside of the Mennonite Church cocoon. I enjoyed that all-around education, learning other things. The teachers that taught it were really good. Mary Oyer taught art and music. I'm not an art and music person—not one to play an instrument or things like that—but Meryl and I used to join the symphony programs in Little Rock and go each year. We enjoyed listening to it.

Gladys and Olive Clemens as students at Goshen College.

With Faith and Persistence

Getting to Know Meryl, Getting to Know Arkansas

After I came back from college, I went to work for Dr. Paul Nace, a Mennonite doctor who had a practice in Souderton, Pennsylvania. He had hired another girl Edith who was an aide, but he needed a nurse and asked if I would come and be his RN. Dr. Nace had grown up just about the third house below us in Blooming Glen. His parents were Lutheran, but their boys became Mennonite.

So I went to work for Dr. Nace. Dr. Thuma (who was now married to Ardys) was working for him at that time too. He was out of medical school and internship. He worked several years with Dr. Nace. Dr. Thuma and Meryl had gone to Goshen College together, and then they roomed together at the Brethren in Christ mission in Philadelphia when they were both going to medical school. Thuma was Brethren in Christ.

I felt like I got to know Meryl better with Thuma telling all these stories about what they did. Meryl was overseas at that time, in Ethiopia and Indonesia. Because of working with and talking with Dr. Thuma, I felt I knew Meryl before he even came back.

After Meryl came back to the United States, he went to York Hospital in central Pennsylvania for surgery residency. He would come home some weekends. We used to have youth meetings at church where young people would present essays. One night we had youth meetings, and he had one essay and I had another one to speak there at church. So Meryl called that afternoon. He said, "I see we're both on the program. Why don't we get together afterward?" I said, "OK." By that time I think Thuma had put in his ear, "Why don't you get to know Gladys?" Working him and telling him, "You should get together."

So from there we just started dating and getting to know each other better. He was getting surgical training at York, and I was in Souderton working. Some weekends he would come in; some weekends I would drive out to York on the Pennsylvania Turnpike. One of my friends in nurse's training, Flossie, had married Harold Bucher, and they were living near York. I'd stay with them. Then we'd date at their house or do things around the area. It all worked out fine.

Bulletin for the Blooming Glen Mennonite Church evening service where both Gladys and Meryl were invited to "give a topic." Meryl said to Gladys, "I see we're both on the program. Do you want to go out afterwards?"

That was in September 1951 when we had our date and got back together. By July we got married. We were married July 5, 1952 in the Blooming Glen Mennonite Church, and I carried daises in my wedding bouquet, my favorite flower. We honeymooned at Lake George in northern New York and Arcadia National Park in Maine.

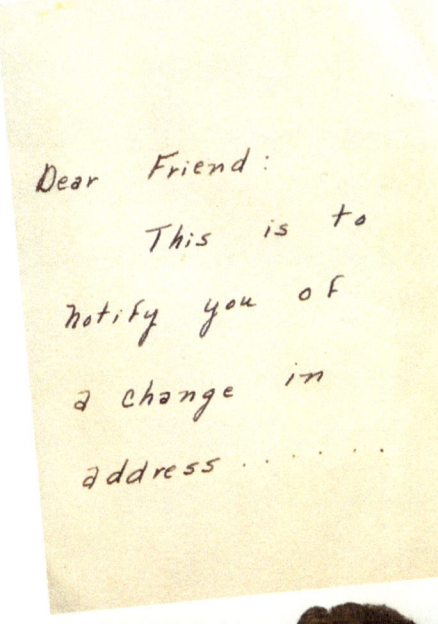

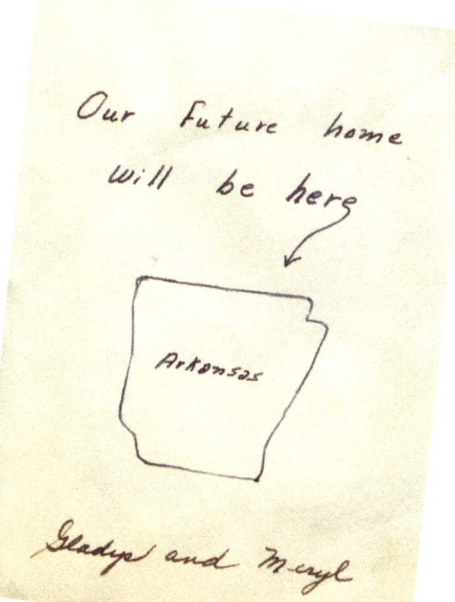

Above: Meryl and Gladys announced their engagement on April 1, 1952. Left: Meryl and Gladys were married on July 5, 1952. Below: Blooming Glen Church on their wedding day.

Consecration Service for Meryl, Gladys, John, and Mary Margaret going to Culp, Arkansas. May 8, 1952.

A month later we went to Arkansas! I had always thought after Goshen College maybe some time I would go on the mission field. That wasn't too difficult then when Meryl wanted to go to Arkansas. It was sort of like a mission field.

The way medicine was practiced at that time in Pennsylvania, family practitioner physicians had to turn their patients over to internists when they went to the hospital. They couldn't take care of their own patients in the hospital. Meryl had in his mind that he wanted to work where medical care was more needed. When we were dating, we went to West Virginia to visit a Mennonite doctor we knew who had started working in a rural area. We looked at his setup to get an idea what it was like in a more undeveloped area.

I think the minister at Culp, Arkansas, Frank Horst, found out that Meryl was looking for a rural place, and he invited him to come out there to work in Arkansas. That happened even before he went overseas to Ethiopia. Meryl and his dad went out there and looked at this area. I think Meryl told him then, "If you don't have a doctor filling in here by the time I return, I'm interested in coming here." That's what he had in mind.

One of the prominent Mennonite physicians at Goshen had gone to Arkansas to visit the mission work at Culp. He discouraged Meryl from considering Arkansas. He said, "You don't want to go there. You won't make a living there! They're so poor they don't even feed their hogs. When I asked, 'What do you feed them?' they said 'We just let them roam, and they eat acorns.' You're not going to make it down there. I don't advise you to go." But Meryl didn't listen to him. And he should see us now! After living here for more than 60 years, we know his thinking was skewed.

We didn't go to Arkansas with the idea of building a hospital. We went there to start a clinical practice, you know. But I always tell Meryl that "if you had known we were going to build a hospital when you proposed to me, I would have said, 'No way. I'm staying here. We won't be able to do that.'" So it's good you don't know what's ahead.

We were planning to settle in Melbourne, Arkansas, because the hospital was there. When we got ready to move from Pennsylvania to Arkansas, we learned that Dr. Karr Shannon had already come to Melbourne. So we went to Culp first to live and then moved to Calico Rock when we found a place to rent.

In Pennsylvania we got Mayflower to come and give us an estimate, and we hired them to move our things. We drove to Arkansas. The Mayflower truck didn't arrive until 3 weeks after we did! Mother Grasse sent a little frying pan for us through the mail with just a tag on it.

I'd never seen Arkansas before we moved there. I remember when we were travelling out I said, "As long as there are hills, I know I'll like it. I don't think I could live in a flat land."

What things cost on our drive from Pennsylvania to Arkansas in 1952: $9/night lodging; breakfast $2.75; ice cream 15 cents; supper $1. We bought a watermelon when we got to the state border, and it was yellow! We'd never seen a yellow watermelon. It was good. Even people in Little Rock had never seen a yellow watermelon.

I can't remember having that hard an adjustment to a new place because we were so busy setting up. The first month we had to find a place to live. When we first got there we stayed upstairs in a clinic over across the White River, in Culp. Two mid-wives lived at the clinic because people didn't cross the river that much. The White River is just on the edge of the town of Calico Rock. The

Near left, Walter, the ferryman at Chessmond Landing; rear left, Miff Sexton, who we often picked up on the way to church because we went right by his house; right, Meryl Grasse.

ferry was the only way to cross the river, and a lot of people in Calico hadn't been on the other side of the river. Then Meryl and I would cross the river to look for a house in Calico. When the river was too low for the ferry to go, we'd have to cross over in a boat.

Above: Joel, Karen, Mark on Chessmond Ferry across White River, circa 1959.

Left: Each Saturday a grocery store in Calico Rock held a drawing for $50 cash as a way to get people downtown.

Below: White River and Calico Rock Bluffs.

Setting Up A Medical Practice

The town of Calico Rock was built on solid rock, and many homes didn't have bathrooms, since it was difficult to install a town-wide sewage system at that time. (In later years, this was accomplished.) With having to set up a medical office, we needed a place with a bathroom. There were only two houses that had bathrooms that we could rent. One of them was too small, so we didn't have much choice.

The property we rented was owned by the Mixon family who were from the area but lived in Texas. There were three little apartments in it. Our apartment was two rooms: a kitchen and one other room that served as bedroom and living room and everything else.

We paid $75 a month to live there. People wondered whether we were buying the place because we were cleaning it up. We said no. They said, "If you're not buying it, why are you cleaning it and fixing it up?"

When Meryl's brother, John, and his wife, Mary Margaret, came to Arkansas, they lived in the second apartment. The people from Texas wanted the third one available for if they came back, but they never did.

There was one other big room that Meryl used for his office and a wide L-shaped hall—at least six foot wide. We used one end of the hall for the waiting room. Later on we put the x-ray over in this L-shape and put a curtain there.

Then we needed to furnish the house and the office. We went to Little Rock to a used medical equipment place and bought a table and things for the office. We didn't have that much

Mixon House, Meryl and Gladys' first home and clinic in Calico Rock, Arkansas, 1952.

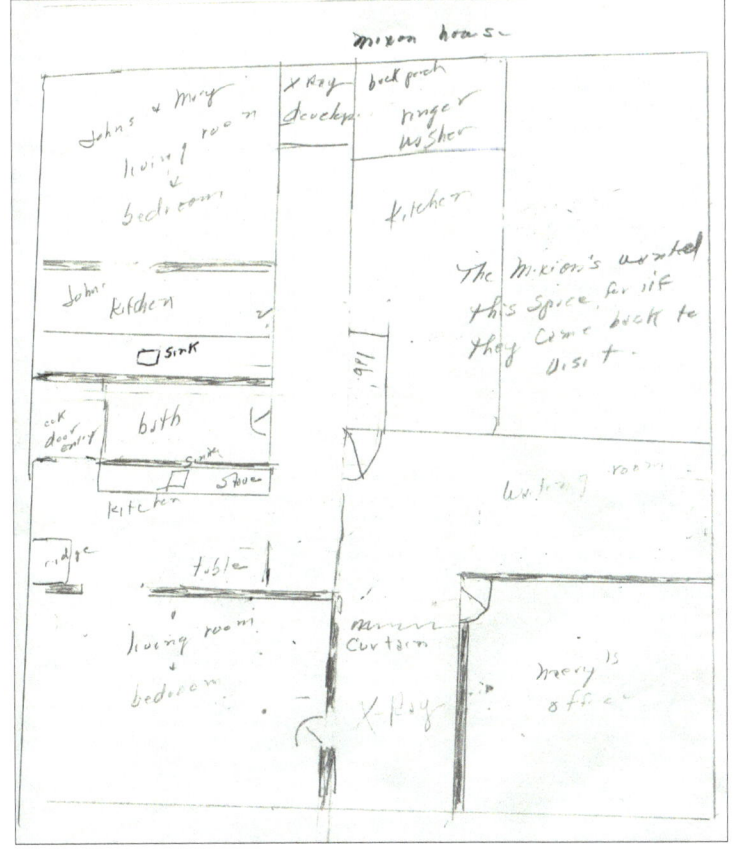

money; we each had a thousand dollars. So I bought the household things, and Meryl bought the medical things.

From then on we were on our own, starting with one patient, two patients. We opened the office in September 1952. You didn't have to advertise in that little town! Even now everybody knows everybody, and word soon spreads. We marked down each day how many patients we had. "We're increasing. Oh, we're doing good! We got enough money to pay the electric bill!" And those people got up early. It would be like six o'clock in the morning and we could tell someone was coming up the steps to the clinic because the house kind of shook. We were in bed yet.

The biggest adjustment was getting used to people coming through your house. There were 13 steps up to the waiting room, but my kitchen was on the level in back, so anybody who couldn't come up steps had to come in through my kitchen. I think they liked being able to see where we lived.

We had one bathroom for all of us. We had to share the bathroom, John and Mag and us, and share it with the public. The other bathroom was in the third apartment, but the owners wanted it for their use if they came back. That part took a little adjusting to.

We had to dry x-rays and gloves in the bathroom that was also used for the public, so we always had to knock on the door to make sure nobody was in the bathroom. When John came to set up the lab, we took all the things out of a closet across from the bathroom and made a little alcove for him to sit in. That was his lab in that hallway between the two apartments.

We moved to Arkansas in August 1952, and in November that year Dwight Eisenhower was elected President. On election night I was listening to the election, and Meryl was out on a house call. The doorbell rang. I thought it was a patient after hours. I opened the door, and who stood there but both our parents! I didn't know they were coming out!

They were concerned about us, how we were doing out there, so they decided to drive out. It took them two days. Just down the hill from us was Wiseman's Motel, little cabins, and they were staying there. When Meryl came home, he was surprised too.

That's when Meryl's mother saw how busy we were getting. Meryl wanted a good medical laboratory and his brother John had agreed that he would come out and help with the lab when we were busy enough we could support two families. So Mother Grasse went back and said, "John, you get out there. They need you right now!" John and Mary Margaret came on Thanksgiving Day and moved into the second apartment in the house.

We had our first child, Karen, while we lived at that place. I often laugh about that: to have a child yet, with just one room and a kitchen! The one room was our living and bedroom. In the kitchen when we sat at the table, between Meryl and I we could reach the stove, refrigerator, and sink without getting up. That's when we decided to look for land to build on.

The second year, Meryl surprised me at Christmastime. In the gift he gave me, he drew a plot of land and said we're going to purchase this land and build a house there. He and John had found two acres on the edge of town. In Pennsylvania a lot of doctors had their offices in their houses. We thought we would do the same—build a house and a clinic, so we wanted more than two acres. But everybody said, "You're fortunate to get two acres! Other people wanted to get land from the seller, and he never would sell it. Don't complain."

The land was on a hillside, and that's where we built our house. We lived on the main level, and the clinic was in the daylight basement. We lived at that house for forty-some years.

Ephraim and Mamie Landis, with granddaughter, Karen Grasse, in Blooming Glen, Pennsylvania, 1954.

New house and clinic on Highway 56, Calico Rock, Arkansas. 1957.

Parenting

Meryl was in a single medical practice for a number of years. If we went to Little Rock, we had to call back to see if anybody came in, in labor. If they had, we would have to turn around and come back. I would never want to go back to that. That was the hardest, I think, in our marriage—the single practice. I knew Meryl couldn't help with child care; he was busy all the time. So I mostly had to be the disciplinarian and all that.

Our first child, Karen, was born at the Melbourne Hospital. When I went into labor with our second child, Joel, we were ready to leave for the hospital, and Meryl was called to the clinic for a patient. After he got home, Meryl helped to put my coat on, and I couldn't walk. Meryl said, "Lay down on the couch, and I'll get my home delivery kit." It was a cold November night, and there was a nice fire in the fireplace near the couch. Karen was about two years old, and she came out of her bedroom and said, "Oh the baby came out." Meryl called Mary Margaret Grasse to stay with Karen, and we went to the hospital with Joel. If we had gotten in the car, I probably would have delivered half way to the hospital in the car.

When I had Joel I thought, "Oh, I know how to raise a child. I had one child. I know what it's like." Oh, no, each one's different! I couldn't use my same methods. I had to learn new parenting all over again. That was a big shock to me.

When we had just Joel and Karen, I would help Meryl when he went on house calls at night. We got to see the county that way and knew where people lived. We put a board in the back of the little Plymouth we had and made a bed there. I put on the kids' pajamas, and then we'd take them along. They'd go to sleep there, and we'd carry them in to their beds after we got back.

They didn't have any nursing homes in the area. The closest one was in Little Rock. So often one of the unmarried sons would stay home and take care of the parents. And Meryl would make house calls. After the parents died, then the son would get married.

My siblings and I were born about six years apart. My sister was at least six when our twin brothers were born, and I was 12. There were so many years between us that my sister and I never became close friends until we were in our later years.

Meryl and I had our children about two years apart because I wanted them to grow up together. I know my mother didn't approve. She was a little shocked that we were having that many children and close together. When I became pregnant with Gwen, it was unplanned. She was born when the twins were seventeen months old. It was a little hard for me to adjust to that. I decided not to tell my mother until the last month, because I knew she'd roll her eyes and say "Why?" I thought she couldn't do anything about it then anymore!

But I'm glad it worked out that way. They grew up together and did things together; they entertained each other. The only thing I regret is that Karen, the oldest one, never had many dolls. We always had babies. I regretted that I didn't let her play more. I depended on her, and she was too young to do that. When I had the twins she would sit beside me and hold a bottle. She was only about six. We had six children within seven and a half or eight years. Karen was always like a second mother in the family to them, and she is now yet.

Our kids' favorite babysitter came to us soon after the twins were born. A girl named Martha Marchant and her mother, Gussie, ran the telephone switchboard for the town. At night they slept beside the switchboard. One took care of the switchboard in the daytime, and the other one at night. They'd take turns.

Our number was 5-0, and they were our answering service when we went on house calls. We'd come back from house calls at night and ask Martha and Gussie, "Did anybody call?" "Yeah, so-and-so called in, and this is what's wrong with them. They wanted to know what to do."

The twins were born December 15, 1959 and Martha came and told us, "I always liked babies. I'd like to learn to help you." She was in high school, about a junior at the time. My birthday is January 17, and as a birthday present, Meryl hired Martha to help me. I taught her how to feed the twins and how to take care of them. She became our kids' favorite babysitter. They would say, "Always get Martha!" Sometimes she'd make a cake in the shape of a rabbit and bring it for them when she was going to babysit.

Martha never married. If she had married and had children, she would have been a great mother. When the telephone office closed in Calico Rock, she went up to Mountain Home and worked for the phone company there. She would always want to see our kids when they came back.

In her later years Martha built a new house for herself. Previously she had lived in her mother's house, after her mother died. Well she had backache and was going to the chiropractor. When they couldn't help her anymore she came to our doctors at Calico Rock. They did surgery and saw that there was cancer all over.

She said, "Can't I just go one night in my house?" She never made it. She died in our hospital. That was October 2012 when I had knee surgery, so I couldn't go to her funeral. Two of our children were home because of my surgery, and they got to go to her funeral. I was glad they could attend.

I didn't have regular nursing duties when the children were young, not until they went to school. But because we had the office in the basement of the house, I was answering the door downstairs all the time. Running down there and answering when Meryl was not around. In the morning he'd do surgery at the county hospital at Melbourne, about twenty miles away, and he had office hours in the afternoon. For a time he started office hours at night, like they did back east. But doctors didn't do that here. So we gave up night hours and did house calls.

I remember one time when Meryl was doing surgery, they brought a man into the clinic who had gotten in an argument with his neighbor, and the neighbor shot him. He was dead! Another time, a barn door had fallen on one guy, and Meryl was at the Melbourne Hospital. The guy was in pain. So I just gave him Demerol, trying to do what I could. Those were the things I dealt with in the clinic when Meryl wasn't around, and I was also responsible for our children upstairs in our house.

One day when we were in Pennsylvania on vacation and Dr. John Grasse (Meryl's cousin who joined the medical practice later) was filling in for us, he called and said the Melbourne Hospital had suddenly closed. The doctor that was there just left. John said, "What shall I do? We've got babies to deliver." So Meryl said, "You've worked overseas; just do them at the house there in the basement, and keep them 24 hours."

So I don't know if Dr. John had to, but after we got back we did that—delivered babies in the basement of our house and kept the mothers 24 hours. I made their meals and did the laundry. I tell you what, it is not easy doing laundry for obstetrics (OB) patients and their babies in addition to laundry for your own family. So I was doing that, and then when they stayed 24 hours, I slept downstairs near them at night. Meryl was upstairs with the children. We had two children at that time.

Meryl had a nurse Carrie Smith, RN, who was his office nurse and took care of the OB patients in the daytime. She was the only RN in the area. When we came to Arkansas in the early 1950's, the only nursing schools in the state were one in Little Rock at Baptist Hospital and one at Fort Smith, western Arkansas. Then there was one at Memphis, TN, which is three or four hours drive away, and Carrie went to Memphis for her training.

A Hospital is Born

After a year we thought maybe the Melbourne hospital would open again. It didn't. We said we can't keep doing this! We knew we had to do something, either stay there or move somewhere else. A place in Minnesota wanted us to come there, but we turned them down. We felt like we were supposed to stay in Arkansas, and we decided to build a hospital.

We drove and looked at Hill-Burton hospitals in Kansas—that's when they were building little hospitals all through the country with money from the

Left to right: Edna Wallace, receptionist; Regina Kauffman, RN trained at La Junta, Colorado; Carrie Smith, RN, clinic nurse; Audney McNeill White, receptionist and later first LPN; Amelia Miller, dietician; Willie Dixon, laundress; Grace Augsburger, RN trained at La Junta, Colorado, director of nursing; John Grasse, lab technician and later administrator.

Hill-Burton Act of 1946[11]. I guess we had somebody fill in for us—Dr. John Grasse, or there was a Dr. Gunthner from Gassville, Arkansas that we got down sometimes after he retired, and he helped out.

We looked at these little hospitals that got government funding and decided we're not going to get government help because then you're obligated to them. We decided we would borrow money and try to build on our own.

We got ideas and sat down and drew plans. We got 13 acres of land. There were two little houses on the land. One was a little white house, and we thought we could make that the hospital until we built. The other was a little green house and it was initially used for nurses' quarters.

It was 1959 and Registered Nurses (RNs) were not available locally because, as I mentioned, there were only two nursing schools in all of Arkansas and neither was nearby. We reached out to Mennonite nurses from other states to come work with us.

The Mennonite nurses who came to Arkansas were Grace Augsberger, Regina Kauffman, Mary Ellen Stutzman, Geraldine (Geri) Bechtel, Arvilla Gingerich, Lois Landis, Jody Hunsberger, Dawn Hunsberger, Betty Peachy, and Peggy Otto. Mary Ellen Stutzman was the Director of Nursing for 25 years. She provided a caring, Christian environment for the hospital. Staff and patients respected her

---

11. Congress passed a law in 1946 that gave hospitals, nursing homes and other health facilities grants and loans for construction and modernization. In return, they agreed to provide a reasonable volume of services to persons unable to pay and to make their services available to all persons residing in the facility's area. The program stopped providing funds in 1997, but about 150 health care facilities nationwide are still obligated to provide free or reduced-cost care. [http://www.hrsa.gov/gethealthcare/affordable/hillburton/]

Mary Ellen Stutzman, RN, held the role of director of nursing for 25 years. Here she is working at the original nurses' station.

immensely. She cared for patients with empathy and often seemed like a chaplain in her role.

Later when community colleges developed nursing programs in Arkansas, we could hire local nurses to staff the hospital and clinics. Audney McNeil, a Licensed Practical Nurse (LPN), was the first locally-trained nurse who worked in the hospital.

At the same time we were making plans for a hospital, somebody told us that the Mennonite nursing school at La Junta, Colorado was closing and the nurses there were looking for jobs. Grace Augsberger and Regina Kauffman decided to come. I say it was the Lord's leading; everything was falling into place.

Grace was great. She wrote all the procedures for the different departments. We got approval from the Arkansas State Board of Health to set up a hospital in the little white house. The house only had four rooms! We had to put a special floor in one back room for the Operating Room (OR.) The Board of Health only approved it because they knew we were in the process of building a hospital.

We could have three patients. The nurses did 12-hour shifts in this little white house. But then there was a time we had five patients, like on cots in

Edna Wallace working at the reception desk as patients wait to be seen at the hospital.

Gladys' Story

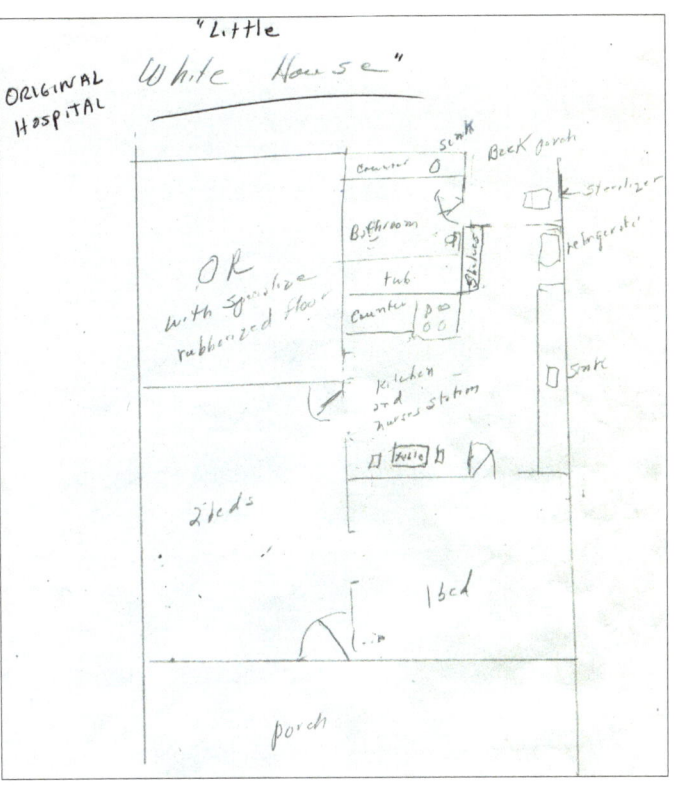

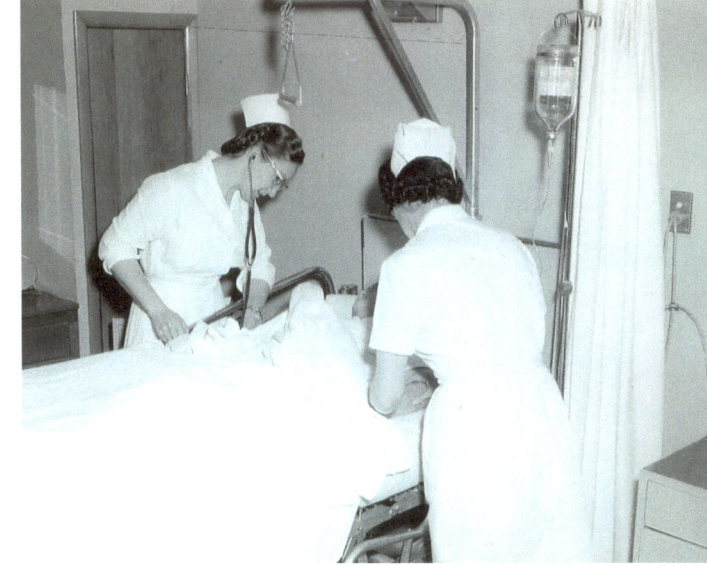

Above: The baby incubator was in the top right of the Operating Room, next to what's labelled "Counter." Top right: Mary Ellen Stutzman (left) and Audney McNeill care for a patient. Right: The Little White House, first hospital, 1957.

Meryl and Gladys purchased 13 acres with two small houses. The white house served as a hospital with 3-4 beds. The green house was a nurses' home.

between. The nurses made the meals and took care of the patients. They had one nursing assistant to help.

Mark, our son, was born there. And Meryl didn't keep me long, not even for 24 hours. I said, "I don't want to go home to three children. I want to rest!" He said, "Well, we need the bed; you gotta go." Later, Chloe, Carol, and Gwen were born at the new hospital we built.

We had a local lady who did the laundry on the back porch. And we had a little entry in the back porch that had a sterilizer. Another lady, an aide, helped with the meals so the nurses could focus on surgery and taking care of the patients.

People were doing home deliveries yet. Access to medical care involved travelling long distances in rural Arkansas in the 1950s. Meryl did a few home deliveries, and always had a sterile kit ready, but most deliveries were at the Melbourne hospital, 20 miles away. People who went to Kansas looking for work would come back to Arkansas to have their babies.

In one case a family brought a baby to us that was born at home. The baby was premature and weighed less than 2 pounds. The family didn't know what to do. They brought it to our little white house and said, "Can you do anything to help it?" Fortunately we had gone down to Texas and gotten an incubator, and we had this incubator next to the OR. Grace thought the baby should be sent to Little Rock. Meryl said, "No, she will get more loving care here than in Little Rock." They didn't have big intensive wards in that time for babies. We put the baby in the incubator and cared for her, and she survived.

One of our hospital maintenance men who polished floors into older age said it was his sister that had that baby. He said he remembered coming into the little white house and visiting that baby. She's grown and married now and has her own family.

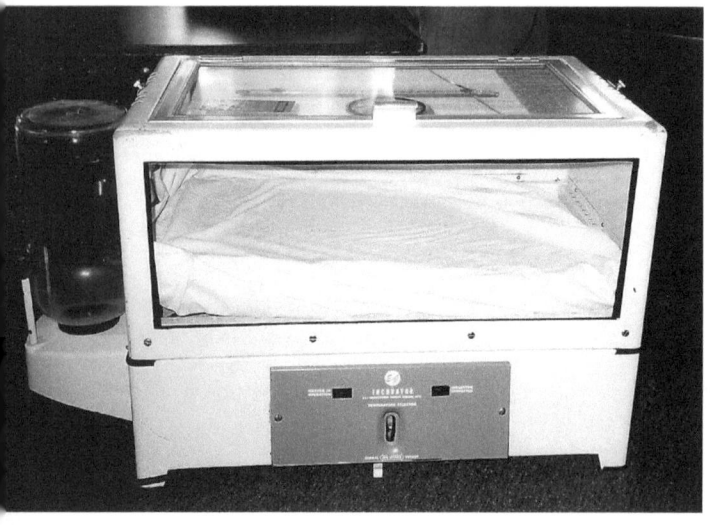

Practicing medicine in "The Little White House." This incubator helped a baby girl born weighing less than 2 pounds survive.

We had decided not to take government funds to build the hospital, and the local bank wouldn't loan us more than five thousand dollars, which was a lot of money in the 1950s. So we didn't know where to borrow money.

Clarence Horst, who was a minister in a rural Mennonite church at Mountain Home, Arkansas said, "I know somebody who could loan you money." There was a guy from Kansas, a big wheat farmer, that came down to help with Bible school at Mountain Home. He wanted to be a minister, but he became a good wheat farmer instead. And then they found oil fields on his land later on.

Roy Selzer, Kansas wheat farmer who gave the first loan to build the hospital. He visited Arkansas various times to help the Mennonite churches and with their Summer Bible School.

We drove out there to Kansas to see this farmer, Roy Selzer, and to ask him if he could loan us funds for a hospital. We drove in there, and he had an old car, and the place didn't look wealthy. I said, "Meryl, I don't think he'll loan us money. He doesn't look like he's making money." But he did. He said yeah. I think Selzer loaned us $20,000. I have a picture of him, because we were so grateful to him.

When we needed to borrow money later on—for the steel and whatever they were going to deliver—Clarence Horst named another wheat farmer that had good money and said, "I think he'll loan you money." The second guy promised us but at the last minute backed down. He had decided to buy more land.

They were ready to deliver this material for the hospital. Meryl said, "We don't have the money. They're going to deliver this, and they won't lay it out there for us." So he called his dad. His dad did have a little money but he suggested, "Why don't you call Grammy Landis?" (Bertha Landis, Meryl's maternal grandmother.) I think my dad loaned us some money later on too.

When Meryl's grandmother gave him her money, he said we'd pay her back. But later on when we went to pay her she said, "No, no. Don't bother." She came out one time to visit and saw the hospital. If it hadn't been for her, we would not have been able

Medical Center of Calico Rock opened in 1959.

Right: First hospital building and sign, circa 1959.

Some of the work team from Blooming Glen, left to right: Paul Godshall, Ephraim Landis, Mamie Landis, Blanche Moyer, Bill Moyer, 1958.

Other members of the Blooming Glen work team, left to right: Ray Histand, David Derstine Sr., Anthony Grasse, Paul Meyers, Lee Moyer, Lamar Hagar, 1958.

First hospital staff, 1959. Left to right: Dr. Meryl Grasse; Edna Wallace, receptionist; Regina Kauffman, RN trained at La Junta, Colorado; Carrie Smith, RN clinic nurse; Audney McNeill White, receptionist and later first LPN; Amelia Miller, dietitician; Willie Dixon, laundress; Grace Augsburger, RN trained at La Junta, Colorado, director of nurses; John Grasse, lab tech and later administrator.

to continue building the hospital. We broke ground in 1958 and opened the Medical Center of Calico Rock in 1959.

Our nearest hospital for major medical procedures was at Little Rock. But at our small rural hospital, Meryl did all kinds of things. He even pinned hips for a while (surgery to fix a broken hip.) We did a radical neck surgical procedure one time on a man who had cancer and refused to go to Little Rock. We got a surgeon to come up from Little Rock, and Meryl assisted him.

We took care of an aortic aneurysm for a patient who didn't want to go to Little Rock, and we brought a surgeon up from Little Rock for that procedure. I was working in the operating room at that time, and I lost sleep over that. Could we handle it? Would we have the right instruments when they came? It worried me. So we were doing some procedures like that. Local people often refused to go to Little Rock.

Mountain Home had a small hospital like us, started by a local doctor, Dr. Benjamin Saltzman, who served as the town's first doctor. The people from our town, before we came, had their babies there sometimes. But the husband had to go out to the restaurants and get the wife's meals and bring them in because the hospital didn't provide meals.

Dr. Robert Lane came to us as a medical student in the 1960s for a clinical rotation from the University of Arkansas for Medical Sciences (UAMS) on weekends. After his internship, Meryl asked him to join him and be a partner. Meryl asked him to get training in anesthesiology, since he especially needed someone to administer anesthesia for surgeries. Meryl had taught his brother, John, to do it. I think he was relieved when Dr. Lane moved to Calico Rock in 1970 and took on anesthesia at the hospital. Dr. Lane is still working there.

We had a number of young doctors that stayed with us for a while, but their wives did not enjoy the remote rural area. Dr. Lane's wife, Sharon, had grandparents that lived at Flippin, Arkansas. They would come up to visit Sharon's grandfather. Then his brother Dr. John Lane eventually came to the town as a dentist, along with his wife Laurie.

We also had numerous medical student preceptees that came for about 6 weeks, for experience in rural healthcare. They lived in our house in the basement apartment.

Nigeria Experience

In 1964 our family went to Nigeria. We traded places with Meryl's cousin Dr. John M. Grasse. (This is so confusing in their family: Meryl had a brother John, a cousin John, and an uncle John!) His cousin, Dr. John, started a rural health program in Nigeria that they wanted to continue. There was a French doctor lined up to come and replace him, and she didn't arrive. When Dr. John got back to the States he thought the program was going to fall through. He couldn't go back because he had already signed up to study psychiatric medicine in Topeka, Kansas.

So Dr. John came through here alone one night and stayed with us. He said, "Meryl, if you go over and continue the rural health program, I'll stay here and

Grasse family just before moving to Nigeria, 1964. Left to right: Mark, Chloe, Meryl, Gladys, Gwendolyn, Karen, Carol, Joel.

take care of your medical practice so that you can go to Nigeria. I'll delay doing my psychiatric training." He said, "I need to know by morning if you will go." We said, "We'll let you know." We had six kids! We prayed about it. In the morning we said, "OK."

John didn't have his wife Betty along when he came for the visit; he hadn't told her yet what he planned to do. So you can imagine what a surprise that was to her! That was in January 1964. Dr. John and Betty, with their children, came out then and lived in our basement while we were getting ready to go to Nigeria. I was so happy for that, because I was packing trunks and Betty was a big help to tell me what to pack and what not to.

By May we were ready to be shipped out. We went over by freighter ship. First we went back east, and the Blooming Glen Church hired a bus to take people from the church to see us off at the shipping dock in New York City. I have pictures of that. We were on the ship a couple days before we left and could watch them loading cars into the freighter to take to political leaders. They were the only ones, politicians, over in those African countries that were getting cars.

The trip was interesting, and the kids just loved it. They only took twelve passengers on a freighter, and we were eight, so we were the only passengers plus one other lady and the crew. We went to the captain's table every day for meals, full-service, and the steward served each one individually. The captain was so worried about the children, didn't want them to fall overboard. One day the ocean was rough, and Chloe's chair fell over backwards at lunch. She was about five years old at the time. He was so worried that she was hurt. They made sure the chair legs were secured to the floor.

Bethel Springs Mennonite Church, Culp, Arkansas, held a farewell party as the Grasses prepared to move to Nigeria, 1964.

Photo credit: Mennonite Board of Missions. Photograph Collection, Arkansas Rural Mission, 1950–1970, IV-10-7.2 Box 2 Folder 6, photo #02. Mennonite Church USA Archives— Elkhart, Indiana.

The Grasse family traveled on the "Corneville" ship from New York City to Port Harcourt, Nigeria in 1964.

Excerpt from letter written on the ship by Gladys to her parents and Meryl's parents (full letter is on next page):

April 15, 1964; Dear Folks,

After you left the dock . . . Meryl and I watched them load some more cargo. They loaded about eight cars . . . without a scratch, also loaded two road scrapers, and a crane in the hold). The long shoremen worked overtime until 7:00 pm so our ship could sail that night.

Eating at the Captain's table makes them [our children] more conscious of their manners. The meals are wonderful. Being Norwegian, they have fish and cheese on the table at every meal. I wish you could see how beautiful they serve the meals. Just like a magazine.

We arrived in Abiriba, Nigeria after travelling 4 weeks by ship, stopping along the coast of West Africa at ports of several countries to deliver cargo. We lived in Nigeria for almost three years. Initially we thought we were going to send our children to school about thirty miles from us, but that didn't work out. So the five older children had to go to school 500 miles north at Hillcrest School in Jos. That was harder on us. I think if we'd known that, we wouldn't have gone! But things just work out.

Joel and Karen both had an initial adjustment scholastically because the Hillcrest School was excellent academically. Mark was in first grade. Chloe and Carol, the twins, started first grade two years later. They were teaching French in third grade already. U.S. AID people were also sending their kids to Hillcrest.

Meryl and I decided we were going to go visit our children in Jos the first semester. It was the rainy season, and the roads were very muddy. The Abiriba hospital administrator told us not to go because we'd get stuck. But we were determined to get up there to see our kids. We had a little VW, and it's good we had that because the weight of the motor was in the back. We made it, but we saw these lorries (British English for truck) getting stuck all along the way.

Initially just the three oldest children, Karen, Joel and Mark, attended school in Jos. We decided to send the three youngest, Chloe, Carol, and Gwen, to the local Nigerian school near our house where they wrote on slates and wore uniforms. When Chloe and Carol turned six and began to attend Jos with the three older children, Gwen had a big adjustment to make because suddenly she was an only child. The first teacher the three girls had at the local Nigerian school was good, but she left the position when she married. The school then got a male

A. MERYL GRASSE, M. D.
Calico Rock, Arkansas

Residence Phone - 130   Clinic Phone - 20

Wednesday
April 15, 1964

Dear Folks!

After you left the dock, we bedded down all the children for a nap and they all slept soundly until 5:00 P.M. While they slept Meryl & I watched them load some more cargo. Around 4 P.M. they loaded about eight cars — this was interesting to see them do without a scratch, also loaded a tractor, two used europeans and a crane into the hold. The longshoremen worked overtime until 7:00 P.M. so that our ship could sail that night. After 7 P.M. they closed the hatches and lowered the booms, and by 8:30 P.M. we started moving out of the harbor. New York looked pretty at night, and also saw Statue of Liberty at night. Children went to bed late so they could watch skyline disappear.

The crew is all very young. Captain Bleiesen has two children — one is 20 months and he has never seen it. His wife just spent 3 mos with him on the ship but children are not allowed to go along, and wife only allowed to do this occasionally. Also engineer & First mate are young with young children so they all fool a lot with our children. These three men sat with us and also at dinner time the Liberian girl who is the only other passenger beside our family. Our meals are served at 8:30 A.M. 12 noon & 5:30 P.M. So far our children have done fairly well at the table. Eating at the Captain table makes them more conscious of their manners. Usually freighters do not employ women. But Norwegians do have some women among crew. There are four on boat who help serve meals & clean rooms. I tried to speak to one and she spoke very brokenly "No speak English".

The meals are wonderful. Being Norwegian they have fish & cheese on table at every meal. Many times they are sardines and even our children love them they really feast on them. I wish you could see how beautiful they serve the meals. Just like a magazine & they are seasoned well. At noon we have such a big lunch & then they serve us dessert. At night we always have soup, main meal and dessert. Bread is homemade

teacher that was very harsh with discipline. One time when the male teacher was real harsh, Nnenna, our house girl who was 14 at the time (and is now like a daughter to us), went and took Gwen out of school. Nnenna said, "Gwen is not going to go to school there anymore."

Gwen picked up pidgin English[12] from playing with her friends in Nigeria. When we came back to the States everybody said, "Why does she talk like that?" She grew out of it soon. Our children enjoyed their Nigeria experience.

In Nigeria, house boys and house girls cook and do household chores in people's homes. They earned money to attend secondary school. John worked as our first houseboy. Then we decided to hire house girls, since boys usually got educated first, and we thought girls should have a chance at education too.

Our first house girl was named Mercy. She worked for us until she had enough money to go to a girl's school. Then there was a young fellow, Ude, who worked in the hospital pharmacy, and he came one day and said he knew a girl, Nnenna, who would like to work in our house. We hired Nnenna. She came to work for us when she was about 14. She was just a year or two older than Karen.

After leaving Nigeria in December 1966, we travelled through Europe before we came back to the States. Our parents were a little unhappy that we weren't getting back in time for Christmas, but we wanted to tour Europe. We landed in Rome, Italy first and immediately bought winter coats and boots. We rented a little VW microbus in Germany and drove through Switzerland and France. Karen had enough French to get us through France. The kids remember that trip—how they had the barn attached to the house and how we slept with the down blankets in a German *gasthaus*. We spent Christmas at the London Mennonite Centre in England, which provided housing for international students, and we sang Christmas carols in the "tube" (subway.)

After we left Nigeria, we didn't have connections with Nnenna for a number of years. Ruth, the Abiriba hospital administrator's wife, came to visit us in Arkansas and said, "Do you know that Nnenna and Ude Eni"—they had gotten married by then—"are in Springfield, MO, at the Evangel Assembly of God College?" The Pentecostal Church was popular in Nigeria, and they were Assembly of God. When we'd go to Hesston College with our kids, we'd go through Springfield, so we stopped in and looked them up. We've been connected ever since.

Nnenna and Ude had two children then, but they'd left them in Nigeria with her mother. After they got their education here, they brought the children over,

---

12. Pidgin English is an auxiliary language that has come into existence through attempts by speakers of two different languages to communicate; primarily a simplified form of one of the languages.

and they'd come down at Christmas and visit us. Nnenna is like a daughter. She calls us "Mummy and Daddy." She comes to our family reunions now. She's just a part of our family.

One time when Nnenna was pregnant with their fourth child, and Ude went to Nigeria to take clothing back to make money in the summer, she came to stay with us. She delivered her baby at our hospital in Calico Rock, and he is thirty years old now! Ude didn't get back right away for them to go back up to Springfield because somebody stole his passport.

The school year was starting, and we decided to put the children in school in Calico Rock until they could return to Springfield. Ubani was in third grade, Eke was a little older, and Chichi started first grade; Ebe was a baby. One of the teachers, Mary Margaret's niece, had moved to Calico Rock from Goshen, Indiana. She said, "That Chichi is going places. She is really knowledgeable for first grade."

Chichi ended up earning full scholarships to college and she works in biomedical engineering. All of Nnenna's kids are like that—high achievers.

When Nnenna's children enrolled in our school, they'd never had black children in the school before. But one teacher sat with some of the children and talked to them about how to treat each other respectfully.

In later years our children always talked about how they liked their overseas experience in Nigeria and they wanted to do it some time again. We went to the Dominican Republic with Christian Medical Society and worked for a week. Karen was in college then; she was doing her Study-Service Term in Haiti. Our other children came along to the Dominican Republic. They joined a group that entertained village children with Christian activities and songs. Meryl and I joined a group that did surgery in a mobile unit.

We did surgery from morning until late at night that week. We were tired. But these people who never had surgeons close at hand came in for surgery. They brought a lady in who had been in labor I don't know how many days. The other doctors with us were solely surgeons. Meryl was a surgeon who did obstetric deliveries. The patient didn't want a C-section, and Meryl said, "I think I can deliver her." He helped to turn the baby and bring it down. She would have died if he hadn't been there, because the other surgeons had never done anything like that.

Meryl liked to travel, and I had never been further than the New Jersey shore until I married Meryl. Over the years we traveled to National Parks in the western USA every 2 years for summer vacations with our six children and a pop-up camper. Internationally, we traveled to Canada, South Africa, Ethiopia, Europe, the former Soviet Union, China, Haiti, Dominican Republic, Paraguay, Mexico, India, Machu Picchu, Peru, and Java, Indonesia.

With Faith and Persistence

Mennonite Church in Calico Rock

When we first lived in Calico Rock, we were going across the White River to the Bethel Springs Mennonite Church at Culp, taking the ferry. We had brought several Mennonite nurses in because there were no local nurses due to there being only two nursing schools in the state. The Bethel Springs minister said "There's enough of you medical personnel over there to start a church." But we didn't want to take too many people out of Bethel Springs church.

While we were away in Nigeria, a bridge was built across the White River in the early 1960s, which made travel from Culp to Calico easier. They didn't have the ferry anymore.

Meryl's brother John and his cousin Dr. John and some others met together sometimes in Calico. Just like once a month. After we came back from Nigeria they said now there are enough families—you three families—and nurses. The minister encouraged us to start a church.

Meryl and his brother John bought a church building up on the hill, the old Baptist church that had been a printing press for a while and deteriorated some. We started a church that met each Sunday in Calico. We served as Sunday school teachers and led the services until we got a minister.

Above: Bridge crossing White River, Route 5, at Calico Rock, built 1964. Left: Photo taken in 2014 from the Route 5 bridge shows lumber from the former ferry dock decaying in the White River. The minister said if the church didn't hold out at Bethel Springs, they could just drive over the bridge and come to Calico then. Bethel Springs church is still active.

Calico Rock Mennonite Fellowship started in the Old Baptist Church in 1967.

Dr. John went up to Goshen, Indiana, one time and met Gordon Schrag who was living there. He had been a minister in a mission church in New York and had moved to Goshen for their children's education. The kids were grown. I don't know how Dr. John met him, but he told him about Calico.

Gordon Schrag came here in his older age and helped start the church at Calico. He and his wife, Laura, were here for a number of years. They related well to the people. Even after they left and went back to Harrisonburg, Virginia to live with their daughter, they came back for the dedication of the new Mennonite church built later in Calico. We'd always let them know by mail how the church was doing.

Our Parents' Later Years

Our parents never finished high school, except for Meryl's mother who got an education and became a teacher. In later years, after her children got out of the house, she went back to teaching. She was one of the first Mennonite women who worked as a teacher—outside of the home—after they had a family.

She would have loved to teach longer, but Meryl's father retired. He said, "Lillian, I'm retired, and we want to do things together." She gave up teaching then because he wanted her to be home more so they could do things together.

My mother, Mamie, wanted to finish high school but her mother died when she was a sophomore. Her father wanted her to stay at home to take care of the house and work in the mill as a bookkeeper.

Mamie and Ephraim Landis following his brain tumor surgery.

My father was diagnosed with a brain tumor when we were living in Nigeria. I knew he was falling at home a lot. He'd fall in the bedroom behind the door, and Mother couldn't get in to get him, to pick him up, so she'd have to call the neighbors for help. They thought it was mini-strokes.

Then somebody said they knew of someone who went to Geisinger Clinic, in Danville, Pennsylvania. My father went to Geisinger for testing, and they found a brain tumor behind his ear. They said it was benign, it would grow very slowly, and it probably wouldn't affect him much. But when he was on the operating room table, he coded and they had to revive him (cariopulmonary resuscitation for cardiac arrest.)

He came home for a while, and it was hard for him to walk. He gave up after that. He didn't have that many hobbies. It was working at the mill, chickens and rabbits—that was his life. It was hard for Mother. If we would have had the rehabilitation we have now with physical therapy, he might have gotten back to walking.

We had him in Arkansas for a little while, and we got him to walk short distances. When we'd make him walk he would say, "You don't love me. You're making me do all this stuff." So finally he went to the Rockhill nursing home in Sellersville, Pennsylvania, for ten years. Mother would go over and feed him every day.

Because Mother didn't drive, she had to get somebody to take her to the nursing home every day. She decided to sell their home, and she moved to a little apartment at Rockhill. That made it much easier for her to go over and take care of Dad and feed him every day.

Mamie Landis in her apartment at Rockhill.

Mother was learning to drive when I was in about fourth grade. It was winter and my parents and another couple went out to Harrisburg to the Pennsylvania Farm Show. It was snowy and my dad was driving. He was coming down a hill, and a car was parked along the road with its door open and a man standing at the door. The man had been getting chains out, to put them on the tires. My dad slid and slammed into the back of the car, and the door closed on the man and killed him.

That was such a shock to my parents. And Dad never got over that, that he had accidentally caused a man's death. My mother said, "I'm not going to drive," and she wouldn't take any more lessons. But in later years she regretted that.

When he was in the nursing home and she had to get somebody to take her, she said, "I regret that I stopped learning to drive."

Homes We Built

We lived at the first house we built in Calico Rock for forty-some years. We bought 50 acres on the edge of town, and Meryl said, "Sometime we're going to build an energy-efficient house there."

We built a new house on the 50 acre farm. We thought we were building a nice house for a Southern climate, but in later years we put in double-pane windows and insulated the walls better. We did a lot to it.

We started the house in 1992 and moved in in 1993, and that's where we lived until 2015.

Meryl's Story

Anthony Meryl Grasse
(b. May 16, 1923, d. January 29, 2016)

Grasse Family Name

Our family name, Grasse, is German; it was originally spelled G-R-A-S in Europe. They Americanized it and made it G-R-A-S-S. Then my father looked in an unabridged dictionary and couldn't find the name Grass, so he thought surely the name was misspelled. He did find G-R-A-S-S-E, which was a Frenchman who had a ship under Lafayette[13]. The French were aiding the Americans in their revolution for freedom from the British back in 1776. My father changed his name to Grasse, the French spelling.

He had two brothers, John and Charles, and his name was Anthony. And then there were five girls, Pearl, Anna Mae, Sadie, Clara, and Mary in the family. The three boys changed their name to Grasse, and the girls continued to spell their name Grass. Therefore there's a variation in the spelling of our name, which is probably an insignificant thing.

Grandparents

After my father, Anthony, married my mother, Lillian, they lived with my maternal grandparents John and Bertha Landis. We lived on my grandparents' farm, on the side of a hill. It's one of the earliest memories I have, living there. It was a large house. We lived on one side of the house, and my grandparents lived on the other side. Anything that didn't please me, I would then go to my grandparents for their consolation. Or if we didn't like the food Mother cooked, my brother, John, and I would go over to Grammy's house.

---

13. Francois Joseph Paul, Count de Grasse, born September 13, 1722, Le Bar, France, died January 11, 1788, Paris. He was a French naval commander who engaged British forces during the American Revolution (1775–1783). Encyclopedia Britannica, www.britannica.com.

Meryl's Parents, Anthony and Lillian Landis Grasse

My father wanted to have his own farm, so he bought the farm my paternal grandfather, Anthony B. Grass, owned.[14] The old home place. He bought that place, so we lived there. After we moved there my brother John and I would take turns going down and staying for two weeks at a time with my maternal grandparents. They wanted us down there with them. We were never very much associated with my paternal grandparents (Oliver and Hannah Grass)—my father's parents, but very closely related with my mother's parents.

My father's parents lived near us and we went there to visit them occasionally. My brother and I liked peanuts. One time when we visited them we ate a lot of peanuts. My mother thought we ate too many and was afraid it would be an insult to them. The next Christmas they gave us a lot of peanuts. I think they gave it as a gift, knowing that we liked peanuts, but my mother took it as a personal insult and thought they gave us peanuts to show that we had eaten so many peanuts at their house.

Valued: Education and Religion

Religion and education were both very important to our family. My maternal grandparents said though they could make a living farming, education was much superior to farming for them. Grammy Landis called her husband a "bale wire farmer." She said his brain was not for farming, that he should have been educated.

My maternal grandfather's family had decided to educate only one child. They were poor people, and they picked one child and gave an education to him to become a doctor. He became a physician—Dr. Daniel Landis[15]. He delivered my mother's children and was our family doctor.

Deborah Gehman Landis (2nd wife) and Dr. Daniel M. Landis, Meryl's great uncle. Dr. Daniel delivered Meryl's mother Lillian's birth as well as Meryl's and his brother John L.'s.

---

14. The 1930 US Census shows Meryl's parents, Anthony and Lillian Grasse, living with John M. and Bertha Landis; Anthony Grasse probably bought the house and farm from his grandfather, Anthony B. Grass, around 1930. Anthony B. Grass died in 1930. Source: Ancestry.com

15. Dr. Landis was a brother to Lillian Grasse's father, John Moyer Landis

We went to church every Sunday, Mother read the Bible frequently to us, and we were taught from the Bible a lot, so I think religion was very important to our family. Each day after breakfast my mother would take the Bible and read to us, teach us, read a story. We got to learn the Bible and also to enjoy it and its philosophies and teachings. Our family worshipped at Blooming Glen Mennonite Church.

My mother had been a teacher, so she was much into education and encouraged us to read and was interested in writing and things like that. My father was more about the farm and into learning to do things on the farm. Taking care of animals, feeding the animals. Much different from my mother.

My mother was much more the disciplinarian. She was more demanding about how we dressed, how we spoke, how we wrote. She was a school teacher, so she was used to discipline. My father was easy going. He'd always tell my brother John and I, if we did something wrong—these boys are making too much noise in the back seat of the car—he'd say "I'll spank you. I'll spank you *tomorrow*." He never would administer punishment the same day. So we'd be real good that day. "Dad will forget." Till the next day, he'd forget. We learned that.

We had boys staying with our family that were 'Society Boys,'[16] placed with us by the Children's Aid Society. Children from neglected homes were taken from those homes and put out on farms. They paid my folks to keep these kids. The Society people would come around and visit us once a month to see if the boys were being taken care of properly.

Above and below: Oliver and Hannah Grass, Meryl's paternal grandparents.

Up in Quakertown, they had Society kids there. One of them, Flucky, came to our house. When he came to live with us he was maybe 12 years old, old enough to work in the fields, and we were small, like 3 or 4 years old. He lived about ten years in our home. He was accepted as one of the children and helped with the farm work and all. Later he started his own home in a small town nearby and became a plumber.

---

16. Society Boys—Children's Aid Society of Pennsylvania founded in 1882.

Left to right: Willard Gene Grasse, Lillian Hockman Landis Grasse, John Landis Grasse, Warren Landis Grasse, Anthony Meryl Grasse, Anthony Meyers Grasse, Alvin Kenneth Grasse.

At one time my grandparents had one Society boy Charlie Dalton, and we had one boy Ted Gratz. They'd be outside together, and my brothers and I would throw gravel at them and make them curse. We liked to hear them curse.

My mother came out and said, "Let the boys alone. Stop throwing gravel like that. You shouldn't be doing that." We thought she wouldn't see us, so we went in back of the barn and did the same thing. She saw us do that, and she came out and broke an apple switch, switched us kids, and told us not to be doing that any more. I remember that very vividly. I'll never forget discipline by my mother. She was very much the disciplinarian, trained us and disciplined us the way we should be trained.

Eventually there were all boys in our family: Meryl, John, Alvin, Willard and Warren. My mother's dream was to have a daughter.[17]

---

17. Lillian Grasse's first three grandchildren were girls.

Farm Life and Food

We did a lot of hunting when I was a kid, you know, there in the hills of Pennsylvania. We'd be hunting for food. I had a .22 caliber rifle that I got when I was about 12 years old. I used to go for squirrel and pheasants. I don't think there are many pheasants any more.

I remember the first squirrel I shot. I was so proud of it! I was going to give it to my grandfather, but he said, "Oh no, no. You killed it. You take it home." We'd kill rabbits too. My grandfather had a single barrel shotgun. He shot a rabbit in the squat, and we took it up to the house, skinned it, cooked it and ate it. We'd bring all those animals back, and we lived on the wild game.

Of course we were country people, and we ate country food. A typical breakfast in the wintertime was cornmeal mush with milk. In the summertime we would have vegetables: fried tomatoes and things like that from the garden. Saturday morning breakfast was different. Since the Catholics ate fish on Fridays, my dad would buy the leftover fish from the Acme grocery store for cheap on Friday afternoons, and we would eat fish for breakfast on Saturday mornings.

A creek ran through part of the farm, and you couldn't farm that, so they used it for pasture. Each day we'd drive the cows down there, and they'd eat the grass down around the creek. We had muskrats in and around the creek. They'd trap those muskrats for their pelts which were valuable for making coats.

Did I mention our barn burned? We had a big barn on the farm. It was raining, and my father went to his brother's house to shut their windows on account of the rain. On the way back he saw lightning strike the barn, and it burned down.

The fire killed the horses and all the cattle except one Holstein cow that broke her chain and got out. The cows had chains around their necks, you know. They were chained to their stalls where we fed them. She broke the chain and got out. For years she had scabs on her back because she was burned so badly, but she survived and was a good cow. All the rest of the animals were burned up.

After the barn burned, people gave my father trees, and he took the trees and sawed them up into lumber. Then they hired people from the local town who came and built another barn. My father put lightning rods on the new barn.

Father's War Stories

My father, Anthony, as a young man had been drafted into the military during World War I.[18] His role was to bring supplies to the troops. He said that he had

---

18. Meryl's father, Anthony Meyers Grasse, entered military service July 15, 1918 and was released April 18, 1919, according to draft card. Source: Ancestry.com

With Faith and Persistence

Anthony M. Grasse, WWI, middle row, far right.

become pacifist when he saw the violence of war and killing. He'd tell us many stories of fighting in battle and of people and the methods of shooting and killing. He told about a general he saw shot, who fell into a mud puddle and was drowned. He was not only shot but drowned. He described other stories to us of the war. Many times he'd talk to us about it, but then he'd break down emotionally and couldn't finish his stories.

Huckster's Helper

Before the war my father sold bread for Freihofer's Bread in Philadelphia. A person who sold door-to-door was called a huckster. After the war, and after he and my mother were married, he went back to the same huckster route in Olney. At that time Olney was a new subdivision with dirt roads outside Philadelphia.

To "draw a chicken" was part of the butchering process, and I was better at it than my father, so I did that to help him prepare for the route. I'd take out the organs and clean the neck, craw, remove the windpipe, intestines, and remove the fat gland in the tail. The heart, liver, lungs, and gizzard stayed with the chicken.

He sold a variety of things such as eggs, chicken, pork, garden produce like beans and sweet corn, and angel food cake and sponge cake. My mother, Lillian, made the cakes they sold—angel food cake only takes egg whites and sponge cake only takes egg yolks. He always had early routes because, being a farmer boy, he didn't mind getting up early. When I was about ten years old I went along with him on Fridays, and I'd lay on the meat box and sleep on the way back.

I had a book with addresses of the 95 people on the route, and he let me handle the people that complained a lot. I remember selling eggs for 35 cents or 38 cents a dozen, depending on the size. One day I didn't have eggs to sell and I told a woman who asked why that "it was too hot and the chickens can't lay eggs." She laughed so hard. Then she went out and told my dad, and I was so embarrassed.

I didn't carry that much change, so when a customer would give me a $20 bill I had to run to my dad to get the change. I'd hold the bill out in front of me. One time the black garbage collectors with their huge wagons said, "Put that away. Someone might take it."

My Landis grandparents had a lot of broiler chickens, and I used to go to the Stover Feed Mill (which Gladys' maternal grandfather owned) with my grandfather. His car had a rumble seat in the back, and John and I would sit back there. Gladys' Uncle Erv, who did the bookkeeping, sat at the desk and read the morning paper. That was the first time I saw a big city daily newspaper. I used to read *The Philadelphia Bulletin* there.[19]

Meryl's maternal grandparents, John & Bertha Landis, weighing eggs for sale.

Elementary and Secondary Schooling

We lived in the country in Bucks County. The address was 133 Upper Church Road, Chalfont, Pennsylvania, and we were in Hilltown Township.

I originally went to Green Hill, which was a country, one-room school down over the hill from us. We had to walk a mile. When my father bought the farm and we moved, then I went to school at Chestnut Ridge for a time. The teacher at Chestnut Ridge gave me such large assignments that I used to study until nine o'clock at night. My mother thought it was too late—that the assignments were too much for us, so she sent me back to Green Hill School again.

Meryl reading the newspaper.

---

19. *The Philadelphia Bulletin* was once the country's largest daily evening newspaper, published 1847 to 1982.

House where Meryl grew up.

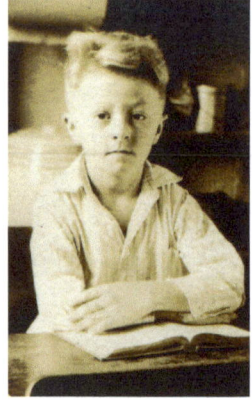

Meryl in elementary school.

Meryl as a teenager.

At Chestnut Ridge School, I recall that at recess and noon hour I spent my time reading books and studying. Occasionally the students would come in and ask me to come on out and play with them, play baseball and things like that. I never especially enjoyed sports, so I did much more reading instead.

The school didn't have a library when I started going there. I thought it was important for a school to have a library. I asked the teacher if we couldn't gather books together and make a library. I said that was important, that we should be able to read and study and learn and have books available. So the teacher and I organized a library for the school. People gave books, old readers and other books, and we put them in the library.

My mother always read many books to us, and she thought it was important that we would read and study and learn because she had been a school teacher when she was young before she married. In fact in later years, in her middle life, she went back to teaching again. They needed a teacher in a private school, and she thought she could go back and teach; so she did. She taught the upper grades: fifth, sixth, seventh, and eighth grades.

My maternal grandparents had two children, that's all they had. Their daughters were Blanche and Lillian.[20] Of course in my father's family there were many children, three boys and five girls. They had a larger family.

They used to ride horses in those days for transportation. We have cars now, but in those times when Anthony M. Grasse and John M. Grasse came to court my mother, Lillian, and her sister Blanche, they came out on horseback. The boys lived further away, on Broad Street, and they would ride horses down to see my mother and her sister. My mother married Anthony, and her sister, Blanche, married John. Sisters married brothers.

My uncle John M. Grasse was a well-educated man and became principal of the high school.[21] Blanche, John's wife and my mother's sister, had been a teacher.

---

20. John M. Landis sent both of his daughters to Millersville Normal School, a teacher's college in Lancaster County, Pennsylvania, after high school. This would have been very forward-thinking to educate daughters in the early 1900s.

21. John Meyers Grasse started teaching in 1918 right out of high school. He earned a BA from Elizabethtown College 1930; Master's Degree Temple University 1934. He was superintendent of Hilltown School District from 1930 to 1956. In 1963 the Hilltown Elementary School was named in his honor, *John M. Grasse Elementary School*, Sellersville, Pennsylvania. Source: Obituary in *Morning Call Newspaper*, May 5, 1992.

Meryl's Story

Barbara Moyer Landis with her granddaughters, Blanche Landis, left, and Lillian Landis (Meryl's mother), right.

She taught me my first year of school. My parents wanted me to get an early start in education, so they sent me when I was five years old. My birthday's in May, so I wasn't six until the May after I started school.

When I was a kid I'd go into a workshop on the farm where they would build things with lumber. I went in and found a tube of glue, tire repair cement, and I walked holding it in my hand. There was a little shed—not the house, but a separate shed—where my grandmother was heating water on the stove. As I walked past the fire in the stove, the tube of glue caught on fire. It dripped down on my leg and got my leg on fire.

My grandmother Bertha Landis was washing clothes there. She saw my pants burning, and she rushed in with her hands and knocked the fire out. She took the glue out of my hand. Her whole hand was burnt. It took several months to heal, so it must have been a deep burn. I'm left handed, and I have a scar there yet on my left hand where I was carrying the glue.

I remember that very vividly, getting burned and her dressing my leg. She said if it wouldn't have been for her, I would have been burned to death. She always told me she saved my life.

I remember they used to dress my legs with lily leaves that had been soaked in alcohol.[22] I suppose the alcohol made the antiseptic. Probably didn't have antibiotics in those days, you know. My leg was burned into the bone, I believe, and it didn't heal until cold weather. So I have a scar.

When I started school I still had a deep burn on my leg. I guess it was a third degree burn. I remember in school I was very small, and they would throw me up in the air, and my leg would go to bleeding and pus would be running. They'd get my Aunt Blanche, and she'd come out. She'd call me in and cleanse my leg and dress it for me.

• • •

For my first three years of high school I went to Hilltown High School where my Uncle John was principal. I always thought that they showed favoritism to me because I was the nephew of the principal. I was in biology and science classes taught by Uncle John. Hilltown High had only three years, so we always had to transfer to another school, to a larger school, for our fourth year. I went to Souderton High School for my fourth year.

I remember the chemistry teacher very well at Souderton High because his pen had come apart and the coat he wore had a big ink stain on the left side. But he always wore that coat! I guess it showed his frugality. He was a good chemistry teacher. I really enjoyed him; I learned chemistry and that probably helped to favor my going into medicine.

I took four years of Latin. At that time I thought it was important to take a language, and Latin was the only language offered. No other languages offered.

I didn't get involved in athletics or sports in high school. I did more reading and studying. I enjoyed that much more than physical activity. And education was very important to me.

---

22. An herbal treatment for burns.

Meryl's family of origin. Left to right, back row: John Grasse, Will Grasse, Alvin Grasse, Meryl Grasse; front row: Lillian Grasse, Warren Grasse, Anthony Grasse.

If I had a free Saturday evening I'd often spend it reading or listening to the radio. We didn't have TV at that time; we only had the radio. So we enjoyed listening to different stories and serial programs. The Lone Ranger and others.

Goshen College

I went to Goshen College, which was in Indiana and was a Mennonite college. There was another church college down in Virginia—Eastern Mennonite College. But I didn't go there. It was very conservative on dress and style. Girls wore black stockings and dressed very simply. They stressed the external aspects of religion. I went to Goshen because my folks thought it would be better.

I was raised with all boys, and when I went to college that was the first time I'd ever associated with girls outside of my cousins. My Uncle John, who was a brother to my father, had girls: Betty and Evelyn and Ruth. Those were the only girls I ever knew growing up. And they had one boy, John.

I never knew how to relate to women, never had any friendships with girls at school. When I was in

Meryl (center) as a student at Goshen College.

Meryl studying at Goshen College.

school, I was really very bashful. I was interested more in doing my lessons and learning and succeeding, pulling A's, being a top student. I liked chemistry and math and physics, those subjects, because I wanted to go into medicine.

I was also interested in earning money, which was important because I had no financial support. My parents didn't support me in college. I saved my own money, paid my own way, I kid you not. My father said I could go, but he wasn't in favor of it. He said, "You can go to college, but I don't especially encourage you to go. You may not turn out well. Your attitude and life will be changed so much." So I went on my own. Later on my father became more accepting of education.

I always hitchhiked to travel to and from college, which was 1,200 miles roundtrip. In those days you could get a ride easily. One time my parents gave me sixty dollars to get a bus ticket to come home. I used the money to buy a single-breasted brown suit instead.

There were like 500 students at Goshen College, and only one person in the whole school had a car. He was a very wealthy person. If you wanted a car, he would rent it to you for an evening. The rest of us didn't have cars.

I had a bicycle because I worked. See they only left me work 22 hours on campus. That was the maximum that we could work. So I worked on the campus, in the library, things like that.

The librarian was very demanding of me in keeping the library clean, so I went downtown and found a job. I had been raking leaves, and this lady recommended me to her husband who ran the plating works that plated the flywheels for Studebakers.

That was a good job. I worked there all winter. They also paid good—we made 35 cents an hour, which was more than I made on the campus. I'd work Fridays and all day Saturday.

We plated those tubular breakfast sets.

And I remember a man fell into the hot water and was burned. I went to see him in the hospital because I had known him. I remember they had painted him with gentian violet—he was blue. I

Newspaper ad for 'modern tubular breakfast set.'

guess he never went back to work, because fifty percent of his body was burned. He probably died from his burns.

I read a newspaper ad about an opportunity to deliver a Packard car from a Chicago dealership to Washington state. The seller could get a better price for the car in Washington, and all the driver had to do was buy the gas to get across the country.

Some Goshen College friends and I decided to drive a Packard to Washington during the summer between my sophomore and junior years and then stay and work in the lumber industry in Oregon for the summer. The pay to work in lumber was $1 an hour, which was much better than the 35 cents an hour you could get in Goshen.

This was during World War II, and I had a 2A deferral from military service due to being a college student. Four of us travelled west together. Paul Lauver was the son of missionaries in South America, so he was a citizen of another country and couldn't be drafted. His girlfriend Betty Yoder was along. Ken Lehman also had a 2A deferral, and when he said he was taking a trip to the west coast, he was immediately drafted. I didn't say anything about our plans to take the trip. I didn't say anything and kept my 2A.

On our trip we went to Salt Lake City to see what it was like. We put Betty in a hotel, and the three of us guys slept overnight on blankets on the Capital Building lawn. In the middle of the night the sprinklers came on!

When we got to Oregon, I worked as a whistle punk. We were working with huge logs. They'd put a huge cable around the log, and then I'd give a signal to

Above: Meryl, Betty Yoder, Paul Lauver on our trip west with the Packard. Right: Salt Lake City, Capital Building.

Delivering Packard, Meryl (center), Summer 1943.

the man at the top to wind the cable to pull the log up onto a big truck. I gained 25 pounds that summer and grew from 5'4" to 5'8".

During my senior year—the 1943–1944 school year—I was editor of the *Maple Leaf,* Goshen College's yearbook. The artists on the yearbook staff were Mary Oyer and Areta Graber. Areta created fraktur, a type of Pennsylvania German art, to serve as section dividers in the yearbook.

1944 Goshen College yearbook staff: Meryl (front row, third from right) was editor. Right: The fraktur artwork, used as section dividers, was created by Areta Graber, associate art editor on the yearbook staff.

Studebaker purchased for $35 to sell yearbook ads.

The student on the yearbook staff whose job it was to get ads bought a Studebaker car for $35 so he could more easily go around and get ads. Harold Bender, college dean, got on our cases about "Where did you get the money to buy that car?" Almost no students on campus had cars at that time.

The cylinders were bad on the Studebaker, but we didn't want to spend money on it. At the local garage they'd put the used crank case oil in a barrel, and we'd go in and take a dip off the top and keep putting oil in the car.

During my time at college, we always sent our good shirts home to our mothers, who did the laundry and sent them back. My mother and grandma

Meryl graduates from Goshen College, 1944.

went together, giving $1 each, to buy me an Arrow shirt. They sent it to me, and I wanted to wear it for Thanksgiving. I pulled the shirt over my head without opening the buttons, and I split it in half! Mary Oyer's mother, Siddie Oyer, who was the matron of the boy's dorm, sewed it up for me.

I had $475 when I started college. When I finished I had a little less than that, a little over $400 that I made in the plating works and working on campus. I paid my own way, and from there I went to medical school.

Hahnemann Medical School

My friend from college, Alvan Thuma, and I went to medical school at Hahnemann in Philadelphia.[23] My mother's uncle, Dr. Daniel Landis, was a doctor, and I went to Hahnemann because that's where he'd gone. Also, it was during World War II, and most medical schools wouldn't accept conscientious objectors to war. Hahnemann accepted anybody, as long as you had good grades. They didn't care what we believed.

There was a Quaker there, Charlie Swift, from Boston. He had been put in prison because he refused to register for the draft. When he got out of prison after six months, he couldn't get into any other medical school. But he was a good student, had the proper grades, so he was accepted at Hahnemann.

A number of us Mennonites were there; we were conscientious objectors to war. Walter Schlabaugh was there, he was a Mennonite. Ezra Nafziger was there. He was a very poor boy. There was another fellow from Michigan that was there.

---

23. Meryl attended medical school at Hahnemann 1944–1947.

Meryl's Story

Meryl's graduating class from Hahnemann Medical School, 1947.

Hahnemann, they accepted anybody. They didn't care what we believed. That's why most of us went to Hahnemann.

There were four medical schools in Philadelphia: Hahnemann, Jefferson, University of Pennsylvania, and Temple. My cousin, John M. Grasse, went to Jefferson. We didn't know about Jefferson.

We thought at the University of Pennsylvania they were more elite and more aristocratic than we were. We were more common people at Hahnemann, poor kids. My daughter works at University of Pennsylvania, but we weren't impressed with them when I was a student.

There was a Mennonite mission on Diamond Street in Philadelphia that was under the Lancaster Mennonite Conference, and Thuma and I checked about living there. They were very conservative and dressed very simply. Blooming Glen Mennonite Church was much more liberal, not nearly as restrictive. We didn't put much emphasis on dress or anything like that. The Mennonite mission didn't think we dressed appropriately, and they didn't let us stay there.

Thuma was from Ohio, and he was Brethren in Christ. We said, "Well, let's go to the Brethren in Christ mission." They were at 3423 North 2nd Street in

Philadelphia. They had bought an empty building next to the church, and they took us in and said we could stay there. They weren't critical of us. One of the things I remember about living there with Thuma is that he wouldn't let me iron our shirts because I didn't iron the tails!

We paid $2.50 a week and lived on the second floor of the building. We ate breakfast and supper there. The woman that ran the mission packed us lunches, and it was always the same: a brown bread Lebanon bologna sandwich and an apple. We ate the same lunch for two years. I remember that. But we were glad to get a lunch, glad to get anything to survive as students.

Later on Thuma and I went to an Italian hospital, and there we got free room and board because we took care of the emergency room for them. The hospital was on 12th and Christian Street, and they had no elevator. When they admitted somebody to the hospital, they had to carry them by stretcher up the steps. I thought it was very primitive.

That hospital no longer exists. I went back there in later years, and we couldn't find any sign of the hospital. I was very disappointed, because it had been an integral part of my life. It was the first hospital I had ever worked in.

It used to be called The Italian Hospital because it was in the Italian part of town. But then when we went to war with Germany and Italy, they didn't think "The Italian Hospital" was very appropriate anymore, and they changed the name to The American Hospital!

There were mostly Italian people there, but I enjoyed living with the Italian people. They had a much different philosophy and a much different lifestyle than the lifestyle I had known. They were more joyful and enjoyed life more.

If a child was born, they'd all gather together and drink whiskey. And they'd forget about the mother—she'd be up in the hospital, you know—but all the family would be gathered together to celebrate the birth of the child! They were a very different culture than I had known, so I enjoyed living at The Italian Hospital. We were there for two years, Thuma and I. Hahnemann was close to that. We could walk to Hahnemann, which was about ten blocks away on 15th and Race Street.

A few other memories from medical school stand out. Our first lecture in anatomy was on the clavicle. Hahnemann was a homeopathic school, and our class always bought the homeopathy professor a bottle of scotch for Christmas. I had the opportunity to assist Dr. Charles Bailey, the famous heart and lung surgeon.[24] He was fearless!

---

24. Dr. Charles P. Bailey was a daring and brilliant thoracic surgeon who pioneered heart surgery techniques at Hahnemann University Hospital in the 1940s to 1950s. He was featured on Time magazine cover in March 1957. Source: Philadelphia Inquirer, Aug.19, 1993.

I wished to develop an interest and become more knowledgeable in theater, music, and the arts because I felt that had been neglected during my upbringing. So while I lived in Philadelphia I went to many operas and regional events to balance out my life and develop interest in that sort of thing. I thought it would be appropriate.

I graduated from Hahnemann in 1947. Mother, Dad, and Grammy Landis came to my graduation which was held at the Philadelphia Academy of Music.

Overseas Service, Then Marriage

When I was in medical school, all the other students were in uniform. They were all part of the Army, were training to be their physicians. We conscientious objectors were in street clothes. I'd seen that they'd given their lives to serve in the Army. I felt I was obligated to serve a few years overseas as a conscientious objector as my service.

The Mennonite Relief and Service Committee[25] sent me to Ethiopia, a very poor country. I was there for three years. A lot of people had syphilis or gonorrhea in that country, and we treated venereal diseases at our hospital. We didn't have penicillin, so we treated syphilis with less efficient drugs. We had 150 people a day.

The Italians had taken Ethiopia, and they had been planning to grow cotton in that area for Italy. They were with the Germans in World War II and had fallen to the Allies and been conquered. We pacifists, our church, took over this hospital. The Italians had cotton gin equipment there from Birmingham, Alabama. We stacked it all aside and made a hospital out of the building for people in the community.

We had ten acres there, and I ran the hospital. I lived in a little house for one person, the manager of the unit. The staff lived in other houses, and we had a house where we ate.

After three years there a church leader came through and said, "You know, I need somebody in Java. You're single. I'll send you to Java." So Mennonite Central Committee sent me to Java, Indonesia

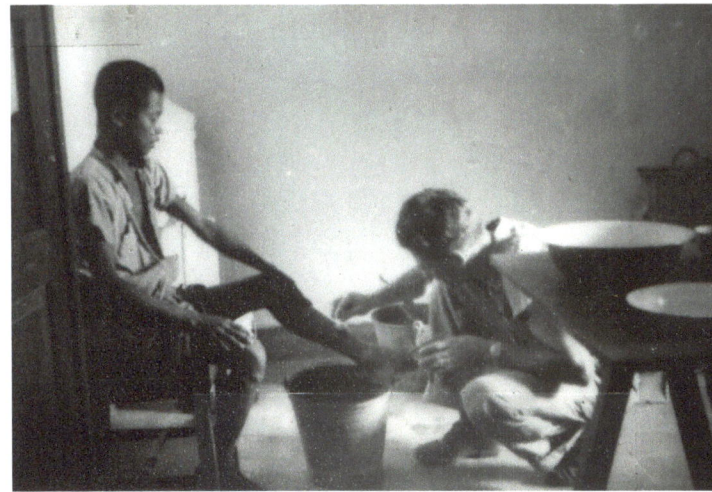

Top: Meryl in Ethiopia, 1948. Above: Meryl with a patient in Ethiopia.

---

25. The Mennonite Relief and Service Committee (MRSC) supported the work of the Mennonite Central Committee (MCC), and maintained relief and service projects under their own administration. Source: *Global Anabaptist Mennonite Encyclopedia Online.* http://gameo.org/index.php?title=Mennonite_Relief_and_Service_Committee_(Mennonite_Church).

Java scenery.

Meryl examining a patient during his service with Mennonite Central Committee in Java, Indonesia, 1950.

for a year. I enjoyed it very much there. It was so different from Ethiopia. They were simple people, happy people. Java is a very beautiful tropical country. It was a great life.

After my year in Java, I came back to the States. I had done surgery before I went overseas, and I thought, "Gee, I sure'd like some formal training." So I went back to York Hospital in Pennsylvania and trained a year as a surgical resident. I worked with the surgeons there and learned their technique to see if I could improve myself.

At that time I knew Gladys, and I was going with her. My friend, Thuma, he had worked for a doctor in the next town, Souderton. He said, "Oh, there's a nurse there you should meet her. She's really a good nurse." I called her and dated with her, and eventually I married her. She became my wife.

I never knew Gladys as a girl, only as a nurse. We both grew up attending Blooming Glen Mennonite Church, but it was a large church, 400 or 500 people. I never knew her in the church.

I said, "I'm going out to Arkansas," and I asked Gladys to go along with me. I didn't want to live back East. I'd been in Ethiopia and Java and I wanted to live where I'd feel more needed and we could have a better life. I thought Gladys would like Arkansas. She says alright, she'll go with me. She'd never seen Arkansas.

I'd been out to visit Arkansas twice before. A friend was teaching at the Mennonite mission school at Culp, so my father and I went out. And one year I went out by myself to look at Arkansas, to be sure that was where I wanted to live.

I liked it because it didn't have the congestion, it didn't have the emphasis on money, it was more casual, more commonplace.

When we first moved to Arkansas, we lived at the Culp Clinic for 2 weeks. Soon, Gladys and I went to the town of Calico Rock to find living quarters that we could use as a clinic too. We found an apartment to rent in someone's house.

We lived in the Ozark Mountains in Arkansas. In southern Arkansas and along the Mississippi River delta was where they had large plantations of cotton. Further south they raised rice, down in Louisiana. We lived up in the mountains.

Back East, they were more interested in their own houses, their own life. In Arkansas the people were more casual and carefree, enjoyed life more. I went out to Arkansas because I had been overseas so many years and I wanted to be more free, have a more easygoing life.

We lived there and made a life there and raised our children. Our children grew up in the house we built on two acres along Highway 56 in Calico Rock. They went to the local school. We tried to give them good moral standards and see that they were well-trained for life. We thought it was important they get their education and go to school. We wanted them to be properly educated. Teach them to love books. Teach them to love animals and birds, plants. Be self-supporting. All those things. To enjoy life. Life is good. You only live it once.

We put a lot of emphasis on religion, Christianity. Important to us. We were pacifists, didn't believe in war, didn't believe you should use war as a way to resolve your problems, so therefore we objected to war completely.

In 1982, my dad died suddenly. I guess he had a coronary occlusion. He was walking to the bathroom and fell over and died. Then my mother was living alone on the farm, so we asked her to come out to Arkansas. She came and lived with us, in our basement. It was a daylight basement where my office was before we built the hospital. My mother was very independent, very self-supporting, self-reliant. She had her own breakfast. Then she ate supper upstairs with us every day.

In 1988, my mother had a stroke and died within an hour in our hospital. She had said she didn't care where she was buried, so we were going to bury her in Arkansas. My brothers objected to that completely, wanting her buried in Pennsylvania with my father. So we sent her body back to Pennsylvania.

Meryl in Java, 1950.

Medical Practice, Calico Rock, Arkansas

When we came to Calico Rock, there was already a county hospital at Melbourne, 25 miles away, but after a while I wasn't satisfied with it. It wasn't well-administered and it closed suddenly in 1956.

In 1957 I began doing surgery and obstetrics in a small house we called the "Little White House." I did my own for years. I was satisfied with my abilities and

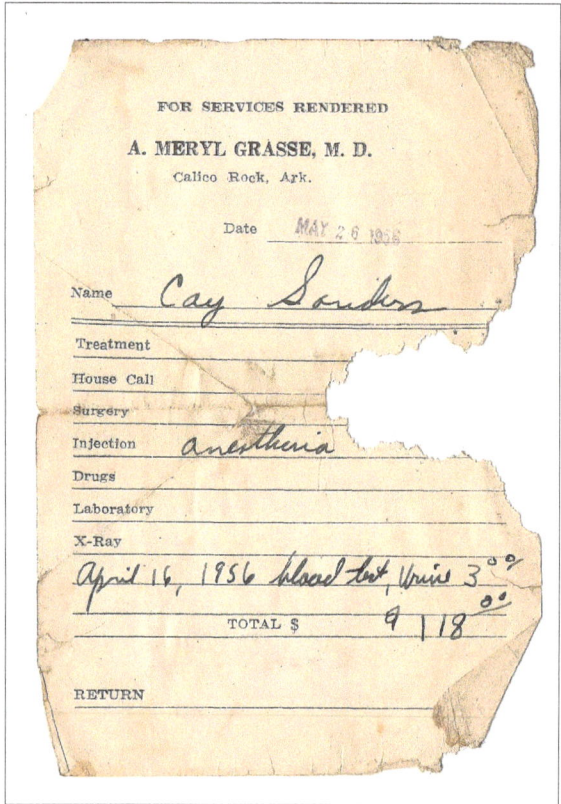

A patient's medical bill, 1956.

Lewis Bell supervised construction of the new hospital in 1959 and multiple additions. Here a new wing under construction in 2006.

felt very competent in my own surgeries. I did a lot of hernia repairs, hysterectomies, all kinds of things.

I wanted my own place where I could do surgery. A very wealthy man from Kansas named Roy Selzer wanted to be a minister, and he came down there to Arkansas, to a local church. He agreed to loan us money so that I could build a hospital. I had good friends that helped to build the hospital: Lewis Bell, who lived near me, and my brother, John. We built a ten-bed hospital in Calico Rock.

I first learned to know Lewis Bell the year we came to Arkansas. I needed a book case for my medical school books, and someone referred me to Lewis who had recently moved back to Arkansas from Kansas.

He supervised the 1959 construction of a new 10-bed hospital and additions in 1969 and 1987. He served as the hospital's maintenance engineer. The hospital, named the Medical Center of Calico Rock, now has 25 beds. (In 1999, it was renamed Community Medical Center of Izard County; July 1, 2017, renamed Izard County Medical Center.) When the hospital opened, my brother John became the administrator. He was trained as a medical technologist, and I had him working in my clinic and hospital laboratory because I wanted a good lab. I always wanted a lab to be accurate and well-done: do blood counts, blood sugar tests, potassium tests, electrolytes.

I trained myself to do everything, to do general medical care: treated diabetes, arteriosclerosis, senility, treated every kind of disease. We had outpatient clinics too, and I enjoyed running those clinics. We set up a clinic at Horseshoe Bend, which was a retirement area where people from Chicago lived. We also set up a clinic at Melbourne. I'd see people there, and we'd bring them into the hospital at Calico to do surgery. I don't recall there was anything I didn't like to take care of. I accepted the challenge of general medical care.

Meryl's Story

Horseshoe Bend satellite office, 40 minutes from Calico Rock.

Melbourne satellite office, 20 minutes from Calico Rock

Robert Lane had come to the hospital as a medical student from the University of Arkansas for Medical Sciences. I told him, "I need an anesthetist up here. My brother John administers anesthesia, but he's not formally trained in anesthesia. I'll use John as a surgery assistant." Lane said he'd go back and learn anesthesia and come back. Dr. Robert Lane arrived in 1970 and still lives in Calico. Later on his daughter became a doctor and joined the group of doctors in Calico Rock. She did primary care, and Lane and I did surgery.

Dr. Robert Lane, circa 1970.

With Faith and Persistence

John L. Grasse, center, assisting Meryl Grasse, near left, in surgery at the hospital.

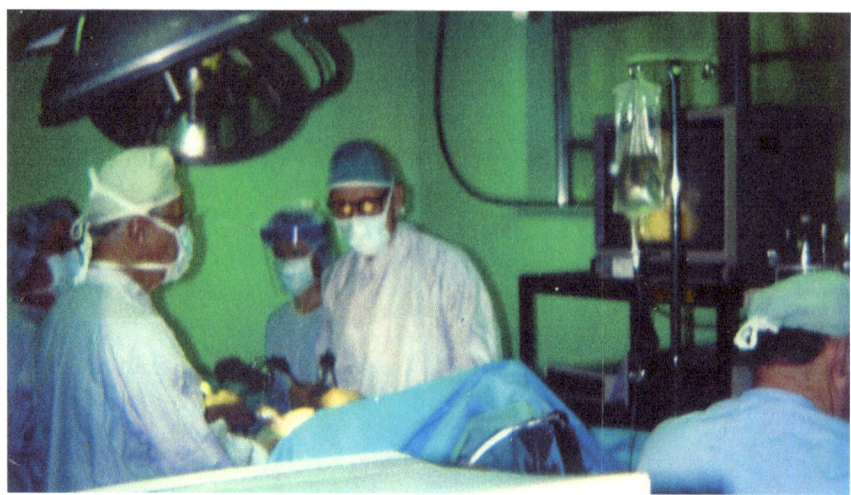

Meryl and his brother John L. Grasse at John's retirement from hospital administrator role in 1990.

In 2003, at 80 years old, Dr. Meryl Grasse performed a cesarean section, resulting in a successful delivery for the mother and this baby.

John Grasse Memorial Garden at hospital.

Later, my brother John died in Arkansas, and we buried him in the cemetery at the old Baptist Church location in Calico Rock, which was also the first location of the Calico Rock Mennonite Fellowship. He and I were very close to each other. I was deeply affected when he died.

Nigeria Adventure

In 1963, my cousin Dr. John M. Grasse returned to the United States from Nigeria and learned his replacement had not arrived. On a visit to Arkansas, he asked me to go to Nigeria for 3 years, and he would work at the clinic and hospital in Calico Rock. I agreed to go to Nigeria with our family to work at the Abiriba Hospital and with the rural healthcare program. We went with the Mennonite Board of Missions, and we worked with the Scottish Presbyterian Mission from 1964 to 1966. Nigeria had gained independence from the British in 1960.

In Nigeria we lived in the eastern region, in the rain forest. The children went to Jos to attend Hillcrest School, which was the only American School in the country. Jos is on a highland plateau—400 feet elevation, which was not very high, but there was not near as much malaria there. The children were put up there separate, 500 miles from our city. We only got to see them like twice a year. Gladys was really homesick to see the children.

Meryl and UNICEF Scout for work in rural healthcare program with Abiriba Hospital, Abiriba, Nigeria.

Letter From The Grasse Family

May 11, 1964

Dear friends,

Tomorrow we reach port Harcourt which makes 4 weeks that we have been on the sea. From New York City we journeyed north for two days to Halifax in Nova Scotia to load many tons of flour, some in 100 pound bags and some in 2 pound bags. We loaded for 2 days at 3 hatches steadily. One day it rained so all rested. There are 5 hatches on this ship. The electric derrick lifts over and down into the hold. The ship and three large electric generators. In one hold is a refrigeration room kept at 35 degrees that contains fruit and Heinz ketchup, ect. We also have a tank for vegetable oils. This trip it is filled with tallow, 400 tons of it, which is kept at 140 degrees. It is for a soap factory at Tema, Ghana. (Check your map or atlas.) The ship carries 5200 tons of cargo which is about the average size of freighters. Of course some tankers and bulk carries (coal, ore, ect.) are 20,000 and even 50,000 tons.

From Nova Scotia we sailed southeast for 10 days decreasing in latitude about 5 degrees each day from 45 degrees at Halifax to 6 degrees above the quator at Abiriba. After two days the sea gulls left us. We saw a ship once or twice hazily in the distance. Rainstorms would come, then the sun. The world seemed empty and void except for our good ship. One mealtime a wave hit the ship and each of us had his glass of water in his lap and Chloe's chair went upside down. We were more than a day from land when we saw the first bird, which followed the ship a short distance, just as Columbus did on his famous journey. Then we saw a flying fish skimming through the waves. One evening we saw dolphins gracefully leaping out of the water. There were probably 150-200 of them leaping 3-6 feet into the air and landing sometimes with a polo. They are mammals as are whales and must surface to breath. We felt we had returned to the land of the living.

Our first stop was Freetown in Sierra (meaning lion of the mountain) and it is a city in a large inlet along a mountainous coast. Most harbors are made of large breakwaters extending out into the sea. We met dugout canoes 3-4 miles from shore, and now we were sure we had reached Africa. An inboard motor boat brought customs and immigration officals aboard and also the shipping agent. Mail was distributed almost at once which included a welcome letter from home. This was the routine procedure at each port. Since the berths were filled, we had anchored in the harbor. The city was out of flour, so barges soon drew along side our ship, the hatches flung open and the derricks began to whine with loads of flour.

The next day the prime minister of the country, Sir Milton Margai, a gynecologist half mast. On the fourth day the barges returned to complete their task, and we lifted anchor that evening.

We passed two ships that had left Freetown earlier and we reached Monrovia, Liberia the next forenoon to occupy the only remaining berth. It was an answer to prayer to get into port so soon. All afternoon and Sunday the derricks labored and men drag raced with the forklifts to unloa the cargo of 500 tons. Since it was Saturday afternoon I could purchase no stamps at the postoffice, but I did find a shop that sold "Time" magazine and also got an African edition of "Ebony". U. S. currency is used in Liberia. We attended worship at the First Methodist Church on Sunday. That night at midnight the cargo was off and we sailed for Ghana.

After two days we reached Takoradi in the evening. We went into our berth the next morning to unload our cargo. We went to town and Shopped in our first Kingsway store. This is equivalent to a supermarket and department store combined. Every sizable town has one. We hauled anchor that evening and arrived at Tema, Ghana at 3 in the morning. This entire port has been built since 1957 for the city of Accra, the capital. We sailed that night and arrived at Lome, Togo in the morning. Here there is no harbor, so the freight was unloaded in dory type boats. Then on to the capital of Nigeria. Lagos is a bustling, shoving, busy city. We had salesman of shoes, jewelery, souvenirs, taylirs to measure clothes and even a barber came on board. The price of a haircut was a pack of U. S. cigarettes. The crew of stevedores worked all day Saturday until 5 A. M. Sunday to unload the cargo because berths were scarce. If a derrick operator would have dozed he would have slid from his perch on the motor 30 feet below into the hold of the ship.

From there we sailed for our destination Port Harcourt which lies up the delta via Niger River.

Sincerely,
Dr. Meryl Grasse

Meryl's letter written on freighter ship trip to Nigeria, published in the Calico Rock Progress *newspaper, 1964.*

Meryl's Story

Excerpt from letter written by Meryl from the ship and published in the newspaper, "The Calico Rock Progress" in Arkansas:

May 11, 1964; Dear Friends,

Tomorrow we reach Port Harcourt (Nigeria) which makes 4 weeks we have been at sea. From New York City, we journeyed north for two days to Halifax Nova Scotia, to load many tons of flour. . . . The ship carries 5200 tons of cargo . . . From Nova Scotia we sailed southeast for 10 days. The world seemed empty and void except for our good ship. Our first stop was Freetown in Sierra [Leone] . . . We met dug-out canoes 3–4 miles from the shore and now we were sure we had reached Africa.

Grasse family being welcomed to Nigeria, May 1964. Left to right: Joel, Karen, Gladys, Chloe, Mark, and Meryl Grasse.

Below: The Grasse children lived in Nasarawa Hostel to attend Hillcrest School, Jos, Nigeria.

They had two seasons in that country: it would rain for six months, then it would be dry for six months. My wife was really anxious to see the children, so in the rainy season we drove up there in a VW to see the kids. The children liked it in Jos because they lived there free and on their own. The school they attended had a house where the children lived and house parents. They had their own rooms. They really liked that independent life, not nearly the close supervision.

Our Land

Later on, after we'd moved back to Arkansas, we got some land from a man who had a flooring mill, oak flooring. That's where we built our second house then in 1992. 336 Red Lane. I had cattle there and horses to ride. We lived in the country—my wife loved that. We had chickens, we had rabbits, we had our own land, our own farm. Had a garden, planted potatoes and tomatoes, all those things.

All of this land I had gotten from this man that had the flooring mill. They used to take the oak, and they'd lay it out in the sun on this land for six months to dry. They'd put it in the kiln and kiln it for two days to 78 degrees. From that they would plane it and make it into flooring.

Over the years, I bought about 800 acres outside of town. The part of Arkansas we live in is very mountainous. This land is up on the hill, in the mountains. We built a cabin, and weekends we go out there.

I planted many acres of pine there that would grow for 20 years. We thought the pine would become valuable for housing material. The year we planted, housing wasn't very good, pine wasn't worth very much. We thought later on the housing would improve and pine would be more valuable. So I planted a huge amount of pine.

The first year all the trees died from drought weather. I replanted them again the second year. I wanted a man that was educated and knowledgeable in forestry in charge of our forest, so I got Jim Schuler to take care of my trees. He was a major in forestry, and he was very knowledgeable. I had him supervise my land, rather than myself. We think it's going to work out; they're still growing.

House at 336 Red Lane, Calico Rock, Arkansas.

Country Doctor Stories

Barter for Medical Care
Oral Story

Dr. Grasse often received payments for medical care in unique exchanges rather than money. One patient gave him a green Jon boat[26] for fishing. He received intricate wood carvings of birds by Gerry and Sherry Chisholm, for delivering their babies. Dr. Grasse told the Chisholms he wanted a carving instead of money. He asked Junior Cobb, a famous Ozark wood carver to bring him a carving when Cobb was not able to pay for delivering a new baby. [Not sure he ever received any carvings. The Smithsonian Folklife Festival 1970 featured Junior Cobb's carvings.] Other payments included beaver pelts, chickens, and quilts.

Bertha's Story
Oral Story

Bertha was an older black woman who lived near the Chessmond ferry landing on the other side of the White River. Dr. Grasse and Gladys tried to help her get welfare for living expenses, but she was denied welfare since she owned several cows and a bare-bones house. So Dr. Grasse gave her a house cleaning job at the hospital in Calico.

---

26. A Jon boat is a flat-bottomed boat with two or three seats for traversing shallow water. Jon boats are popular in the Ozarks for float fishing on the rivers.

When is she going to die?
Oral story contributed by Gladys Grasse

In the 1950s and 60s, the nearest nursing home was in Little Rock, Arkansas, so people took care of their parents or terminal patients at home. One time when Dr. Grasse made a house call visit, a man asked him, "When is my mother going to die?" He told Dr. Grasse that it was getting very costly feeding all of his relatives who had gathered and stayed at his house waiting for her death. He said he could afford the doctor bills but the grocery bills were eating him up.

Kid with a Painful Stomach
Handwritten story

A young man about 18 years old was a long way from home. He was spelunking in one of our caves across the river with a group of young people. He came down with severe stomach pain and shock. The hospital called the boy's mother near Chicago and said he needed surgery immediately.

She was so afraid that her son would be going under surgery at the hands of some backwoods doctor, and besides she was concerned about his care in such a small hospital. She counseled with her pastor about the situation. Not only had he heard about Calico Rock but he knew Dr. Grasse. He had passed through Calico Rock a few months before this incident.

The son had the surgery, and it turned out to be a gangrenous intestine. A partial segment of the bowel was removed, and the son recovered without any complications. Dr. Grasse's partner, Dr. Lane, had given the anesthesia, and the mother sent him a pair of knitted gloves she had made for him.

Thirty years later Dr. Lane searched on the internet and found the man then lived in Washington D.C. He had three young children, and everyone was doing well.

"We Didn't Send a Whole Lot Out"
From news clipping, unidentified publication

Dr. Lane started traveling to Calico Rock as a senior student at University of Arkansas for Medical Sciences years ago. By that time Dr. Grasse was looking for help. The two had to be willing to tackle almost any problem, Lane remembers. When a tough case confronted them, the only choice was "drive 100 miles or fix it. Basically, we didn't send a whole lot out."

Things changed some when Lane took up flying his own single-engine plane. A woman went into difficult, dangerous labor with the hospital about to be socked in by snow. Lane got her into his plane "in the middle of winter, in the middle of the night, and we made Little Rock in 30 minutes." People asked, "What would you have done if she'd had her baby in the airplane?" He says, "I'd have sold the airplane."

Ferryman's Cyst
From news clipping, unidentified publication

Dr. Grasse arrived before the bridge was built that carries Arkansas Highway 5 traffic across the White River into downtown Calico Rock. In those days, the only way to cross the river there was by ferry.

"The ferryman had a cyst on his left eyelid as big as a walnut," the doctor remembers. "He could only see out of one eye." Grasse offered to remove the cyst. But the ferryman said he couldn't pay—said he already had another doctor to pay off.

No matter, Grasse said, and he snipped the cyst for nothing. "Yeah," the doctor says now—"so I didn't have to look at it. I took that ferry all the time."

Reminiscing
The Medical Center of Calico Rock . . . then and now . . .
By Helen Lindley, published July 4, 1996 in the White River Current

It was good to get back home after a week in the hospital. But it's also good to be in a hospital when you need medical care. And, as far as I'm concerned, when I'm ill, I would rather be in the Calico Rock hospital than in a big city hospital. The attention and care you receive there helps a patient recover.

My first stay in the Calico Rock hospital was in 1962 and there had been many changes since that time. I was so impressed by the care, at that time, that I wrote an article titled "The Brothers Grasse at Calico Rock." This article appeared in the July, 1964 edition of *Christian Living* magazine. Today's modern hospital is a far cry from that 8-bed hospital and small staff but the loving care of the doctors and nurses has not changed.

During my first stay, I kept complimenting Amelia, the cook, on her home baked bread. When I was discharged, Amelia presented me with a loaf of her bread. I also remember her scolding me for not eating the liver she had cooked. I said, "I don't like liver." She stood at the side of my bed with her hands on her hips and in a stern voice said, "I don't know anyone who needs liver more than you do."

Another hospital stay I recall was in January during very cold weather. While there, a blizzard began blowing and all traffic came to a standstill. That evening, I began to complain because my husband, Sam, had not come to see me. I remember Mary Ellen Stutzman scolding me. She said, "It would be foolish for anyone to try to make it to town during a blizzard." To entertain the patients, she and two other nurses came around after their shift was over and sang hymns to calm us. It worked better than any sedative.

Since Medicare came into being, the doctors and nurses have less time to spend with the patients but the time they do spend is "quality time." Thank you Dr. Meryl and Gladys Grasse, John and Mary Margaret Grasse for all the years of hard work and dedication to the health and welfare of the people of this area.

House Call: Faith and Medicine
Oral Story

Dr. Grasse: One time they called me and asked if I would come to a home to see a patient. She was very sick, and she came from Kansas City. She said that I had delivered one of her babies. So after hours I went up and saw her. They had a little mobile home that was not very big, with trash thrown around the outside of it. The lady that was taking care of her was a sister to her ex-husband, so she was no kin to this girl at all. A brother had brought her down from Kansas City and had left her there at this lady's house; I don't recall her name. The brother returned to Kansas City.

I talked to her a little bit. She was very apathetic and said that she had a bad disease of her cervix. I realized that she had far advanced cancer of the cervix. She was about 37 years old.

She had wanted chemotherapy, but her mother was a minister who was a faith healer and told her that she could heal her by prayer. In fact, after she was down there, out near Wideman in the mobile home here in Arkansas, the mother came down several days later and said, "Oh, she will get better. We will just pray for her." She lived about 10 days, and then she died.

It showed that cancer of the cervix still can be a fatal disease and also shows the misplacing of faith in dealing with disease of this nature. It also showed the kindness of the family taking her in. They were just happy that I was able to come and let me know the next day that they were happy that I came to see her.

Sharing Food in Appreciation for Medical Care
Oral Story

Many times when Dr. Grasse made a house call the family would ask him to sit down and eat with them. Or they would send food commodities home with him that they received from the government: good cheese, rice, large cans of peanut butter.

One time when he had delivered a baby at home, the family had a big feast set for after the delivery and asked him to stay and celebrate the new baby with this feast. He remembers that during the celebration the mother was in bed in a back bedroom and everyone sort of forgot about her.

Letter to the Editor
January 1, 2004, from local Arkansas newspaper

Dear Editor, The Community Medical Center of Izard County provides exceptional care to the people of this community and the surrounding area. This fact was brought to my attention during my recent hospital stay. I received prompt and courteous care from the minute I walked in. I would like to thank the following people and applaud them for their professional dedication to their jobs: the ladies who work so diligently in the clinic office; Dr. Knight and her nurse who treated me with first class care; the lab people who work swiftly and efficiently to do their difficult jobs; the x-ray lab workers who were friendly and patient; the ladies in admissions who helped me fill out a stack of papers in record breaking time; the exceptional nursing staff (both day and night shifts—I could not say thank you enough for the standard of care they provided); the hospital auxiliary ladies who came by to lend a friendly face and smile; the hospital cooking staff who make hospital food taste like home cooking; and last, but certainly not least, the janitorial staff who keep the hospital so clean.

In the future when the hospital or hospital auxiliary is having a fund-raiser I will be ready to participate in whatever way I can and strongly encourage our community to do the same. We are fortunate to have such an exceptional hospital and clinic at our disposal—friendly faces of people you know working diligently to provide the best care for you. This is what separates CMCIC from all other hospitals. With all my appreciation and admiration. Sincerely, Buffy Russell-Brightwell

Queen Elizabeth Roses
Oral Story

In the 1960s in the back of the hospital a Calico Rock nurse, Scotty, planted three Queen Elizabeth roses against the hospital building. She had also planted three at her house. All of hers died, but the ones at the hospital lived. When we were preparing to blacktop the area against the hospital building, John Grasse, hospital administrator, dug up the rose bushes and planted them at another place. The replantings did not grow. But to our surprise, a rose bush emerged through the blacktop at the hospital! Apparently John did not get all the roots when he moved the bushes. This rose bush still survives—it is about 12 feet tall and bears nice roses each year.

We had an older man as a patient who had no family to come visit him. Nurse Mary Ellen Stutzman would cut roses from this rose bush and place a small bouquet on his bedside table.

Treated in Such a Special Way

> May 6, 2001
>
> Nursing Staff
> Calico Rock Medical Center
> 103 Grasse Street
> Calico Rock, AR 72519
>
> Dear Nursing and Physical Therapy Staff,
>
> Our family would like to express our appreciation to you for all the care and concern you showed for our beloved family member, Hazel Love, while she was a patient at the hospital.
>
> We have all been very favorably impressed by not just the physical care you gave her, but also for the emotional care. To those of you who took extra time to go into her room, hold her hand, pat her shoulder, coax her to eat or drink, and give her kind words of encouragement: <u>Thank You</u>. We recognize that you all had busy schedules and had other patients to tend to, so it is meaningful to us that you treated her and our family in such a special way.
>
> Thank you again for all you have done. It means more to us than you could know.
>
> Sincerely,
> The Love Family
> Ed & Charlotte Love
> Bob & Ellen Love
> Debbie Love
>
> ✓ Cc: Hospital Administrator

Tidbits and Timelines

Gladys

I was the first girl on my mother's side of the family. There were three boy cousins born before me, and they often told me, "We made a tom-boy out of you."

• • •

After I graduated from nurse's training, I served that summer of 1950 as a camp nurse at Laurelville Mennonite Camp.

• • •

My dad was making payments on a powder blue 1950 Plymouth sedan for me. Meryl and I were about to get married, and Meryl had the exact same car. When my dad found out, he gave the Plymouth to my brothers instead.

• • •

When Meryl and I dated, we went to Philly and watched movies. He "led me astray" because in our time going to the movies wasn't allowed. Meryl especially liked to see the foreign films about Africa, India, and other countries.

• • •

We mailed out our engagement announcements, and they arrived on April Fool's Day. Some people wondered if it was an April Fool's prank. They said, "Who are you marrying? We never see you together!" At the time Meryl was doing surgery in York, Pennsylvania, and I was at nursing school in Philadelphia. We'd slip into the back of church when we would both be home on a weekend.

• • •

We took our honeymoon in the Adirondacks at a place called Frontier Village in Lake George, New York. Then we went up to Vermont to visit Mennonites who were commissioned by Blooming Glen Mennonite Church at the same time we were. They were starting a church there.

• • •

Right after we were married, we were sleeping at Meryl's house, and I heard gunshots in the early morning. Meryl's mother, Lillian, told me she was shooting sparrows. This surprised me, because my mother wouldn't even touch a gun.

• • •

Meryl treated malaria cases when we first came to Arkansas.

• • •

There's a dedication stone in the hospital's exterior wall that says "Blessed be God . . . who comforteth us in all our afflictions." I Cor. 1:3-4

• • •

I'd tell our daughters Carol and Chloe: "You twins are alive because of your dad." Chloe was breech and Carol was transverse. John gave anesthesia and Meryl turned the babies and delivered them.

• • •

We didn't ferry across the White River much at the Calico Rock landing, we always went to Chessmond. The Chessmond Ferry cost 50 cents to cross. Harold Funk owned the ferry and hired Walter, an alcoholic, to run it. Sometimes we couldn't wake Walter when we needed to cross to see a patient or deliver a baby. Meryl missed several baby deliveries at the Culp Clinic, so the midwife took care of them.

Meryl

I have a brother Alvin. He's a big hunter, so he went up to live in Canada, and he's been there many years. My brother, Will, he stayed on the home place. Then I had a brother Warren. He lived also back there in Pennsylvania. I didn't get to know Warren very good at all. He was a lot younger than we were. I knew Will better, and Alvin, and John. John lived here in Arkansas. Five of us. Warren was born about 9 years after the youngest brother, Will, and he often said it seemed like he was an only child.

• • •

Meryl's father, Anthony, working as a huckster, wore out two trucks driving to Philadelphia every Friday to sell produce, meats, eggs, and butter door-to-door in the Olney area of Philadelphia. He built his huckster business from the bread route he'd had with Friehofer's Bakery in Philadelphia before WWI.

• • •

I remember my grandparents separating large eggs and medium eggs. They sold them to the other hucksters in Blooming Glen.

• • •

Horseradish hucksters would say "Horse . . . radish!" and if people wanted it, they'd grind it fresh right there.

• • •

During the time Meryl went to Hahnemann Medical School in the 1940s, they only allowed 10 women into every class of 100. Most medical schools in the country had quotas for women, Jewish, and black applicants.

• • •

Al Gaary, a Catholic, was in our wedding party. He went to the Catholic Church and confessed that he was participating in a Protestant church ceremony before coming to our wedding! He was from a Polish family and changed his name from Grabowski to Gaary. I met him in medical school because we were lined up by names alphabetically: he was #54 and I was #55 in our class.

• • •

Meryl served on the Calico Rock city council for 26 years.

• • •

Meryl was part of the group that founded the Mennonite Medical Association in the 1940s, which became Mennonite Health Services and now goes by MHS.

• • •

Virgil Thornley was the Calico Rock ferryman later.

Details from an unattributed article written about Meryl's life:

Meryl was planning to spend 3 years in surgical residency at York Hospital "but was cut short when the local draft board would not recognize his 3 years overseas." The draft board wouldn't let him finish the surgical residency and said he had to serve in a needy area right away.

Meryl and his dad had visited the Calico Rock area in 1948 because the Mennonite Mission Board had started a school for migrant and local children at Culp, Arkansas where they noticed the local medical needs. Culp is 7 miles from Calico Rock across the White River, and the only access was by a local ferry. Meryl decided that, following his overseas service, if there was not a doctor serving the area, he'd return and set up his practice there.

How the Mennonites Were Invited to Come to Arkansas

Maude Douglas was a woman from northern Arkansas who was travelling with her second husband, Ed Buckingham, to Colorado Springs for work when he became ill. He was treated at the Mennonite Sanatorium and Hospital in La Junta, Colorado. Since they didn't have money, Maude worked in the hospital laundry to pay for his care. Ed had cancer, and he died in the hospital.

Maude decided she wanted to be a nurse, but she didn't have a high school degree. La Junta Mennonites helped her go to Hesston Academy (Kansas) for high school, and then she trained at La Junta and became a Registered Nurse in 1929. She also joined the Mennonite Church.

After she received her nursing degree, she returned to Arkansas, married John Douglas, and they bought land and built a home near Culp in 1932. Maude provided nursing and midwifery care to families in the mountain community. She delivered babies in the surrounding area, travelling by mule to hard-to-reach communities when limited medical facilities were available. She asked the Mennonites to come help serve the area, which had very little access to educational and medical resources.

Maude Douglas learned to know Mennonites when, as they were travelling through, her first husband fell ill, was treated, and died at the Mennonite Hospital in LaJunta, Colorado. She became a nurse and invited Mennonites to come to Arkansas to provide medical care.

Many of the families were migrant workers, and the children didn't have the chance to attend school.

Mennonites responded to Maude's call, and this was the beginning of a school, a health clinic, and the Bethel Springs Mennonite Church in the Culp area. As others in the Mennonite Church became aware of the needs, the Mission Board sent additional workers and Mennonites spread out over northern Arkansas.

Maude lived in Calico Rock beginning in 1964. For eleven years she worked as a night nurse at the Calico Rock Medical Center.

Sample of Hospital Auxiliary Activities
Hospital Auxiliary

Trained volunteers for hospital tasks

One activity within the auxiliary was the "Pink Ladies." In the early 70s they began helping in the kitchen during canning season and expanded to other tasks. Pink Ladies took two days of training and learned to do things like make the beds, sterilize surgical instruments, feed patients, visit patients

Fundraising

Fixed up the interior of The Little White House

Hospital Grateful Patient Fund

In August of 1965, Mrs. Ethel Cook of Mountain Home initiated the Grateful Patient Fund. She did this in appreciation of the Christian love and care she received at the hospital. She was hospitalized in 1965 in what was considered by the doctors to be extremely critical condition. She was over 80 at the time and was not expected to live. After lying in a coma for three days, she began a remarkable recovery and was soon able to leave the hospital.

Mrs. Cook died a year later, but during that year she was able to travel and visit her children. It was after her recovery that she set up the Grateful Patient Fund to express gratitude for the love and care she received at Medical Center of Calico Rock.

History of Community Medical Center of Calico Rock

From *A Taste of History: A Unique Collection from The Community Medical Center of Izard County, Calico Rock,* Arkansas. Kearney, NE: Morris Press Cookbooks, 2009.

Aug. 1952	A.M. Grasse, MD and Gladys Landis Grasse come to Calico Rock
Sept. 1952	A.M. Grasse, MD starts office in Mixon House
Nov. 1952	John and Mary Margaret Grasse move to Calico Rock and John becomes lab technician and surgical assistant
1952–1954	Clinic office continues in Mixon house
Jan. 1955	A.M. Grasse, MD moves into new house and office on Hwy. 56
1956	Melbourne Hospital closes and we deliver obstetric patients in our office on Hwy. 56. Carrie Smith, RN is the office nurse who takes care of patients during the day, and Gladys Grasse, RN tends to them during the night. We also keep a few emergency patients who refuse to go to Little Rock for care.
Mar. 1957	Purchase tract of land (13 acres) with 2 small houses, and operate a hospital for 1 year in the Little White House. The green house next door is the nurses' house. The Little White House has 3 to 4 beds. The nurses work 12 hour shifts and also cook the meals.
1958	We break ground for 10 bed hospital.
Jul. 1959	An open house is held for the 10 bed hospital and doctors office on the other end.
May 1964–1966	Dr. Meryl Grasse and his family go to Nigeria, and Dr. John M. Grasse and his family come to fill in at Calico Rock and stay until 1970.
Aug. 1968	Preparations are made to enlarge hospital on each end. New additions include semi-private rooms, dietary, and family room. On the clinic end, the office area is enlarged.
1969	John L. Grasse (Meryl's brother) becomes hospital administrator. The office area and new clinic waiting room is completed.

Jan. 1970	Move into enlarged hospital area. Robert C. Lane, MD joins the practice.
1972	Another expansion area for new doctors and new emergency room and physical therapy
1976	Gary Villines, MD joins the group practice
1982	Home Health begins. Webb Ross, MD joins group practice. Jack Schlosser installs solar power system for hot water on laundry rooftop.
1983	Gary Villines, MD leaves the practice. Nuclear medicine is added.
1985	Louis Campos, MD joins the group practice. Satellite clinic is started in Horseshoe Bend, along with physical therapy department in the clinic.
1986	Webb Ross, MD leaves the group practice
1987	Third addition to the hospital includes 2 x-ray rooms, ultrasound, mammography room, and large physical therapy department.
1988	In the fall, construction begins for eight new private rooms
Sept. 1988	Lloyd Plemmons, MD joins the group practice. Cathy Franks, Diane Jenkins, and Cathy Ward go into nursing school for RN degrees. Gladys Grasse works in place of Cathy Franks in the clinic.
1989	Donald O. Wright MD joins the group practice
1990	John L. Grasse retires as the administrator. Terry Amstutz takes new position. Open house is held for 8 new private hospital rooms.
1991	Hospital comes from being a share-holders ownership to a non-profit corporation and governed by a board of directors. This board in turn approve and hire CEO to administer the hospital.
	Build new clinic at Horseshoe Bend. Open house is held in August. Dr. Meryl Grasse is awarded by Arkansas Hospital Association in Little Rock in October of 1991.

Feb. 1992	Dr. Meryl Grasse receives the Allen H. Erb Memorial Award from Mennonite Health Association in Indianapolis, Indiana for establishing health care in Calico Rock. New Home Health and Hospice building is built.
1992	Dr. Meryl Grasse takes Laparoscopy course in Sacramento, CA. He performs the first Laparoscopic surgery in Medical Center of Calico Rock on July 12, 1992.
1993	CAT scan machine is added to the x-ray department. Hale Home Health moves into their new building.
Apr. 1994	Dr. John M. Grasse retires from medical group.
1995	Melbourne clinic is purchased from Ozark Medical Center in West Plains, MO. In October, Dr. Meryl Grasse and his brother John L. Grasse receive Culture for Service Awards from their Goshen College Alumni Board.
1996	Hospice begins
Jun. 1996	An open house is held for the satellite clinic at Melbourne. Bethany L. Knight, MD and Dewane Brueske, MD join the group practice.
Oct. 1998	Construction is started on a new Melbourne clinic with room for 2 physicians and large physical therapy department. Opens in 1999.
1998	Dewane Brueske, MD leaves the practice and Z.B. Beyga, MD joins the group practice. Babysitting courses begin to be offered.
May 2000	Dr. Brad Mayfield (surgeon) joins the medical group.
2001	New CT scanner is purchased. David Sitzes, MD joins the clinic group practice. The name of the hospital changes from Medical Center of Calico Rock to Community Medical Center of Izard County. In September, Dr. Meryl Grasse and Gena Nave become Co-Administrators.
Sept. 2002	Mobile MRI begins at the hospital. The 50 year anniversary of the Grasse brothers coming to Arkansas and opening the Medical Clinic in the Mixon House is celebrated.

2002	Hospital Auxiliary remodels and redecorates the Little White House. Renee King and Janice Hamby are decorators for the project.
2003	AET Ambulance Service begins. Hospital family room is redecorated and new furniture is purchased.
2004	Reed Mack Perryman retires as hospital pharmacist for 37 years
2005	Dr. Krueger joins clinic staff
Sept. 2, 2005	New heliport pad across the street from the hospital is dedicated
Mar. 17, 2006	Ground-breaking for 16,000 square feet addition
Aug. 2006	Angela Richmond is hired as new President/CEO
2006	NCU Philips Scanner is purchased
Apr. 29, 2007	Dedication of new hospital expansion of operating room, emergency room, reception, gift shop, physical therapy, and nurses station. Dedication of chapel that was furnished by CMC Hospital Auxiliary. The stained glass window was created by Doris Flurey (Mountain View) dedicated and placed in honor of Dr. Meryl and Gladys Grasse by Monroe and Lou Ingram and Dr. Jim and Allison Ingram. The stained glass picture represents the Calico bluffs and the White River. The dove carrying an olive branch represents the Grasse family providing health care to Calico Rock.
May 2007	The "Healing Garden" was a gift to the hospital in the memory of Mrs. Joe (Miss Willie) Matthews by her 5 children, 13 grandchildren, 22 great-grandchildren, 6 great-great-grandchildren and spouses. Miss Willie delighted in taking flowers from her yard and house plants to patients in the hospital. Miss Willie's Garner family (her parents) was among the pioneer families in Calico Rock. As the railroad was being built at the turn of the century, her father and uncle created some of the first store buildings on Main Street of the newly established town. The Matthews, her husband's family, were among the pioneer families of the Pineville community, settling there in the mid 1860s.

Feb. 2008	Tornado destroys Mountain View hospital and doctors use our hospital for patient care and surgery.
Jul. 2009	50th Anniversary of opening of first hospital building in Calico Rock

Dr. Meryl Grasse's Service and Recognition

1967–1993	Served on City Council of Calico Rock
1979–1981	Served on board of White River Area Agency of Aging
1991	Named winner of Distinguished Service Award from the Arkansas Hospital Association
1992	Received Allen Erb Award, along with his brother, John, from Mennonite Health Association
1995	Received Culture for Service Award, along with his brother, John, from Goshen College
1999	Received Key to the City of Calico Rock from Chamber of Commerce
1999	When the hospital celebrated its 40th anniversary, Dr. Grasse and shareholders of the hospital donated the hospital to the Community Advisory Board of Directors as a nonprofit institution
2003	Received recognition from Izard County Retired Teachers Association for health care in Izard County, along with Dr. Harold Tatum from Melbourne, Arkansas.
2015	Received Key to the City of Calico Rock for 25 years of service on City Council
2015	Emeritus Physician Designation (Community Medical Center of Izard County)

Front & Center: Dr. Meryl Grasse

Calico Rock physician still going strong at 86

http://www.arkansasonline.com/news/2009/aug/16/frontampcenter-dr-meryl-grasse-20090816/

By Susan Varno CONTRIBUTING WRITER

This article was published **August 16, 2009**.

Dr. Meryl Grasse has been a driving force in health care in Calico Rock for nearly 60 years. He started the Community Medical Center there and also worked as a medical missionary in Africa in the 1960s.

THREE RIVERS AREA — At age 86, Dr. Meryl Grasse works at least two days a week as a physician and another two days as administrative consultant to the Community Medical Center in Calico Rock. He spends some of his free time raising cattle and serving his church.

"I wouldn't know what to do if I retired, " he said.

When asked how other people can be as energetic and healthy at his age, he said, "We are [discouraged] by the poor diet, increased obesity and lack of exercise of most people."

He and his wife, Gladys, raise their own vegetables and work out on their treadmill, stair climber and arm exercise machines.

In August 1952, Grasse and his new bride arrived in Calico Rock. One part-time doctor and one retired doctor served the area. Today, the multimillion dollar Community Medical Center (CMC) serves the region. This 17-bed Critical Access Hospital includes surgical suites, physical therapy, extensive lab and radiology departments with CAT scan and endoscopy and mobile MRI access. They also have a healing garden, a chapel and a gift shop.

Four or five times a week, a helicopter lands at the helipad bringing trauma victims or transporting patients to hospitals in Little Rock or Springfield, Mo. At the recently expanded 24-hour emergency room, two full-time physicians treat 200 to 300 patients a month from Baxter, Izard, Stone and Fulton Counties. Seven full-time and 10 part-time and consulting doctors staff the clinic with satellite offices in Horseshoe Bend and Melbourne. For the past 50 years, Grasse and his family have been the driving force behind the medical center.

Born in 1923, Anthony Meryl Grasse grew up on a farm in Bucks County, Penn., and attended the Mennonite Church in Blooming Glen with his family. Soon after graduating from Hahnemann School of Medicine in Philadelphia, he received a letter from the Mennonite Church at Bethel Springs in Stone County,

Ark. Pastor Frank Horst told him of the great need for a doctor in the Calico Rock area and asked him to come for a visit. In 1947, Grasse accepted the invitation. He liked the rural setting and wanted to provide good care where there was little medical care.

First the Mennonite Central Committee sent him to Ethiopia and then to Java as a physician for two years. In Ethiopia Grasse helped convert a vacant cotton gin into a hospital. Returning home he renewed his courtship with Gladys Landis. They married July 5, 1952, and with $2,000 they had saved, they arrived at the Mennonite Medical Clinic at Bethel Springs (Culp, Arkansas). She owned a bedroom suite, and he had a car.

In Calico Rock the couple rented a house that had been divided into four apartments. After buying medical equipment in Little Rock, they opened their practice on Sept. 13. Because he was the only local doctor who kept regular hours, patients lined up every day. If he had to go out on an emergency, they waited for hours, but no one ever complained. He treated cases of malaria and tuberculosis, injuries and spider bites as well as hypertension and stroke.

"I wanted a good lab," Grasse said. "My brother John had graduated from Hahnemann as a lab technician. Years earlier I had asked him to join me when I needed him."

Election Eve 1952, both sets of their parents arrived for a surprise visit. When his father returned home, he told John to get ready to move to Calico Rock. John and his wife, Mary Margaret, who was an RN and dietitian, arrived later that month. They moved into the other upstairs apartment, but both couples shared one bathroom.

In those early years, Grasse performed surgeries in the morning at the small hospital in Melbourne and saw patients in the afternoon. Many evenings he and Gladys dressed their children in pajamas and took them along on house calls. While he was away from the office, the town's telephone operator, Gussie Marchant, took his calls for him.

John Grasse administered anesthesia for his brother's surgeries. Afternoons he ran lab tests and operated the 2000-pound X-ray machine stationed in the waiting room. John developed the X-rays in the common bathroom, which were often ruined if someone opened the door. In 1954 the Grasses built a larger house with their clinic in the basement.

"Our patients were faithful about paying their bills," Grasse said. "Some would sell a cow if they had to. We never had to ask for payment."

The Melbourne Hospital suddenly closed in 1956. Grasse began delivering babies at his clinic or at the mothers' homes. In 1957 the four Grasses had been talking about opening a hospital in Calico Rock when a man came to the clinic.

He was in a hurry to sell two nearby small houses on 13 acres of land. That weekend Grasse bought the land without even checking the titles.

The first year they operated the hospital with three beds and two cots in the "White House" and used the "Green House" as nurses' quarters. Most of their nurses were Mennonites who always took the time to cheer patients and to gather in the hall to sing hymns.

Local businesses and residents encouraged Grasse to build a hospital in Calico Rock. Using their own funds and borrowing from their family, the Grasses couldn't raise enough money. Then Mennonite Roy Selzer from Protection, Kansas, offered to finance the rest without a promissory note. In 1958, they broke ground for a 10-bed hospital. Local people and work teams from the Blooming Glen Church helped with construction. The hospital opened the next year.

Christmas, 1963, Grasse's cousin Dr. John M. Grasse came to visit. He said he would take over at the hospital if Grasse would continue Dr. John's mission in Nigeria until a replacement could be found. In May, 1964, Meryl and Gladys and their six children—the youngest was 3—moved to a rural 150-bed hospital. The children thought it was a great adventure. The family had to return to Calico Rock in December 1966, when civil war broke out in Nigeria.

Meryl was hospital administrator until his brother John took over in 1969. The next year the hospital added more beds, laboratory and radiology and began home health care. In 1972 the clinic expanded and an emergency room and a physical therapy unit opened. Several doctors had joined the staff. They formed a group practice in 1985 and opened a clinic in Horseshoe Bend. In 1991 the family-owned hospital became a nonprofit corporation. They built the Melbourne Clinic in 1995.

In 2005, the Hospital Governing Board put up $950,000, borrowed $1 million from First National Bank of Izard County and received a $2 million loan from the U.S. Department of Agriculture. They broke ground for the latest expansion in 2006 and opened in 2007.

As for Grasse's future, he intends to do what he's been doing for the past 60 years, bringing good medical care to people in need.

Matter of Fact—

Birth Day: May 16, 1923

Occupation: Physician

Family includes: All the people I come in contact with, especially my patients

Hobbies: Gardening, farming, photography and tropical fish

My name comes from: I'm named after my father, Anthony Meyers Grasse. My mother said we can't have two Anthony Myers, so the doctor who delivered me, who was also my great uncle, suggested Meryl as my middle name.

Most people don't know: I can make cornbread

I cannot live without: Work

When I was young I wanted: To be educated

What makes me mad: Poor habits of the current generation, obesity and poor diet

The person I most admire: Jesus Christ

My favorite memory is: The functioning of the hospital where I worked in Ethiopia

Three Rivers, Pages 123, 126 on 08/16/2009

Family Recipes
Culinary Tastings Across Cultures

Pennsylvania Dutch Recipes

Chicken Corn Noodle Soup
—*Gladys Grasse recipe*

    1–2 cups diced, cooked chicken
    2 quarts chicken broth
    1 small onion diced
    1 stalk celery diced
    1–2 cups fresh or frozen corn
    2 cups flat egg noodles
    salt and pepper to taste

Cook a chicken prior, debone and dice, save broth for soup; or buy roasted chicken at grocery store, cut up and dice. In soup pot, sauté onion and celery in small amount butter. Add broth and bring to a boil. Add corn and cook until ready, then add noodles and chicken. Salt and pepper to taste. Serve hot.

Tomato Rivel Soup
—*Gladys adapted this recipe from the Mennonite Community Cookbook.*

To make rivels:
    ½–1 cup flour
    1 egg

Rub egg and flour together until crumbly, like the size of a cherry stone. Set aside.

Prepare in saucepan or soup pot, and bring to boil.
    1 large can or jar of tomatoes [diced]
    1 small can V-8 juice

Then put rivels in the soup and cook until thick. Add 1 pinch of baking soda (to prevent curdling when milk is added) and stir to mix in well. Gradually add 1–1½ cups milk and stir in. Ready to serve.

Scrapple
—Meryl Grasse recipe from 2002, 4th revision

> 4 cups cornmeal (Mix in 1–2 cups cool broth before adding cornmeal to boiling liquid)
> 5 quarts broth (pork broth, from cooking the head to make the puddings)
> 2 cups buckwheat flour
> 2 cups whole wheat flour
> 4 cups puddings*
> 3 tsp salt
> 3 tsp pepper
> 4 tbsp sage (fresh or dried and pulverized)

Mix and when boiling, cook 30–45 minutes, until mixture "bloops" (boils slowly). Then pour into prepared scrapple pans and let cool until firm. Turn out on board and cut in blocks for freezing or slice and fry crispy to eat fresh for breakfast.

*Puddings are a mixture of ground organ meats and head meat

Shoo Fly Pie
—Recipe adapted by Gladys from More-With-Less Cookbook

Preheat oven to 375°

Prepare one unbaked 9-inch pie shell

Cut together with pastry blender:
> 1 cup flour
> ½ cup brown sugar
> 2 tbsp shortening or butter
> Reserve half cup of crumbs for topping.
> Combine in mixing bowl:
> 1 cup sorghum molasses
> 1 egg slightly beaten
> ¾ cup cold water
> 1 tsp soda in ¼ cup hot water

Add crumb mixture and beat together. Pour into unbaked pie shell. Sprinkle reserved ½ cup crumbs on top. Bake 35 minutes.

Raised Cakes (Cinnamon Buns)

—by Mamie Baum Stover Landis. Recipe passed to Mamie by her grandmother and through the generations. Gladys, her daughter, passed on the art of baking.

- 2 cups mashed potatoes
- 3 cups boiling water
- 2 ½ cups sugar
- 1 cup shortening (Mamie Landis used Oleo with a small part butter)
- 3 eggs
- 1½ tsp salt
- 8 to 9 cups flour
- 2 tbsp dry yeast
- Softened butter/Oleo, brown sugar, cinnamon (for spreading on dough)

Measure 3 cups of flour and mix all dry ingredients together with yeast. Put shortening into 1 cup of boiling water, then gradually add this and rest of boiling water to the mashed potatoes. Add dry ingredients to mashed potato mixture (which should be 120–160°). Beat for 2 minutes on medium speed of electric mixer. Then add ½–1 cup more flour to make thick batter. Add eggs and beat on high for 2 more minutes. Keep adding flour until it is too thick for mixer. Pour mixture into very large dish (Mrs. Landis used a very large enameled dish pan she kept for this) after adding small amount of flour to bottom of dish to keep batter from sticking, and add rest of flour. Mix in flour until batter sticks together and is light but easy to handle. Flour hands so dough does not stick as you knead dough in bowl or on floured board for 5–10 minutes. Make round ball and place in bowl, cover and let rise in warm place until twice the size. (approx. 3 hours). Then take ¼ of dough and put on floured board or pastry cloth, roll to about ½ inch thickness in oblong shape, spread with softened oleo/butter, then spread brown sugar and cinnamon over it. Roll up like a jelly roll, cut into 1 to 1 ½ inch pieces. Divide into prepared greased pans, allowing pieces to touch each other. Then let rise to double in size.

Bake at 350° for 30 minutes or until golden brown. May ice when cool.

For sticky buns use this topping in bottom of pans then bake:

Topping:
- 1 lb. brown sugar
- ¼ cup water
- ¼ lb. butter/Oleo = ½ cup
- ½ cup molasses (like dark Karo or King syrup)

Bring all ingredients to boil for one minute and cool. Put small amount of topping sauce (⅛–¼ inch) in bottom of pans. You can use this topping or it you prefer, just a good layer of brown sugar in bottom of pan and dot with butter, then place cut rolls on top and bake.

Mocha Pudding
—Adapted by Gladys Grasse from "Mocha Ice Cream" in the Mennonite Community Cookbook

    1 pkg. plain gelatin (about 2 tbsp)
    1½ cup strong coffee (can add ½–1 tsp decaf instant coffee, the stronger the better!)
    ¼ cup brown sugar (can add up to 1 cup if you like it sweeter)
    5 oz. evaporated milk
    1½ cup milk
    1 tsp vanilla
    1 cup whipping cream, whipped topping or vanilla ice cream
    ½ cup nuts, shredded coconut, mini chocolate chips or shaved chocolate—after pudding is jelled, place on top

Dissolve gelatin in cold coffee and let stand 5 minutes. Melt on low heat over hot water until clear. Combine evaporated milk, brown sugar, vanilla and milk. Add dissolved gelatin and mix well (if not strong enough, add more instant coffee). Add whipped cream, topping, or ice cream. Pour into serving dish and place in refrigerator. When partly jelled, add topping and return to fridge.

Meryl Grasse's Peanut Brittle
—Made at Christmas time

    3 cups peanuts (roasted, okay if hulls on)
    4 cups sugar
    1 tbsp butter
    1 teaspoon soda

Have all ingredients ready and measured before starting. Prepare at least 2 buttered cookie sheets to pour candy out on and a heat tolerant spatula to spread mixture flat. Melt sugar slowly over medium heat in cast iron pan until liquid. Quickly add peanuts and butter. Last stir in soda (it will foam) then quickly transfer to cookie tray and spread out flat. Cool in dry, low humidity place. Break up into bite size pieces and store in tight, dry containers.

Springerle Cookies

—German cookie with embossed design by pressing a special rolling pin <u>mold</u> on the dough before baking. Springerle can be traced to the 14th century, a Christmas cookie. Gladys learned this recipe from her college roommate's mother, who was German. A Grasse family favorite.

- 4 cups sifted, confectioners' sugar
- 4 eggs
- 4 cups flour
- 20 drops anise oil (¼ Tsp.)
- 1 tsp baking soda
- 2 tbsp anise seed

Add sugar gradually to well-beaten eggs. Continue to beat for 15 minutes with electric mixer.

Add anise oil and blend into mixture. Combine sifted flour and soda, add gradually and stir until a smooth, stiff dough is formed. Cover bowl and let dough rest for 15 minutes. Chill dough in refrigerator for a couple hours. Divide dough in thirds. Roll dough out on lightly floured board to ¼–½ inch thick. Dust "springerle rolling pin" with flour, and roll on dough to make designs. Press firmly and cut on imprint lines. Place cookies 1 inch apart on lightly greased baking sheet. Sprinkle with anise seed and cover with towel. Let stand in cool place overnight to dry. Bake in slow oven at 300 degrees for about 20 minutes until light straw color. Remove from baking sheets and cool on racks. Makes 6 dozen. Keep cookies in a tightly covered container.

Dandelion Wine Recipe

- 3 quarts dandelion flowers, no stems
- 2 quarts cold water
- 2 pounds sugar
- 1 yeast packet
- lemons sliced

Directions

Pour the water over the flowers and let stand in a large crock for 3 days and 3 nights. Strain through a cloth, add sugar, yeast, and lemon. Let stand 4 days and 4 nights. Strain again and bottle.

ARKANSAS Recipes

Pinto Beans with Ham

    1 lb dry pinto beans
    one ham hock or chopped country ham
    ½–1tsp salt, depending on saltiness of ham

Rinse beans and place in crockpot with 4–6 quarts water. Add ham and salt and cook until beans are soft. Add water as needed so beans do not dry out. Serve with cornbread and sautéed greens. Note: Meryl cooked pinto beans in a pot on the wood stove.

Fried Okra

—Grasse family favorite in summer

    10 pods okra from the garden, sliced in ¼ inch pieces
    1 cup cornmeal
    ¼ tsp salt
    ½ cup oil vegetable oil

Coat okra slices with cornmeal. Heat oil and fry okra until golden brown. Delicious!

Optional: Soak okra in mixture of 1 egg, beaten, for 5-10 minutes; then coat with cornmeal.

Persimmon Pudding

—Persimmon trees are native to Arkansas. Gladys learned this recipe after moving to the South

Mix together in mixing bowl:
    2 cups persimmon pulp
    3 eggs
    1¾ cup milk

Mix dry ingredients together in separate bowl:
    2 cups flour
    ½ tsp soda
    1 tsp salt
    ½ tsp cinnamon
    ¼ tsp nutmeg
    ½ cup sugar

Gradually add dry ingredients to liquid mixture. Then stir in 2 tbsp melted butter.

Pour into greased and floured 9x13 pan and bake at 325° for one hour. Serve cold with a dollop of whipped cream on top of each piece.

Cornbread
—Southern cornbread uses all cornmeal, no flour. Meryl made this recipe.

Beat together:
- 2 eggs
- 1 tsp soda
- 2 cups buttermilk

Mix in:
- 2 cups cornmeal
- 1 tsp salt

Pour into buttered 8" X 8" square pan. Bake at 450 degrees for 20–25 minutes until just set. Alternate: Bake in buttered cast-iron skillet

NIGERIA Recipes

Groundnut Stew
—Favorite dinner at Nasarawa Hostel in Jos, Nigeria where 5 Grasse children attended boarding school. A Grasse family favorite.

- 3 cups (2 lbs.) cooked meat, chicken or beef
- 1 quart broth
- Add and simmer 30 minutes:
- 1½ cups favorite vegetables (potato, onion, pepper, green beans, yam, carrot, etc.)
- 1½ cup chopped tomatoes
- ½ tsp curry
- 1 tsp salt
- 1 tsp parsley
- ¼ tsp thyme
- ½ cup peanut butter (easier if first mixed w/ hot broth/water and thinned)
- Cayenne or hot pepper to taste

Near end of cooking, add ½–1 cup chopped peanuts if peanut butter is not chunky. Serve with hard-boiled egg sliced on top. Serve on hot rice, with side dishes (toppings) of coconut, pineapple, diced fresh tomatoes, chopped peanuts, diced onion, chopped banana, chopped apples, sliced orange/mandarin, sliced grapefruit, raisins, etc.

John's Chocolate Cake

—John was houseboy for Grasse family in Abiriba, Nigeria and Gladys taught him to make this recipe.

    2 eggs
    ⅔ cup cocoa
    3 cups flour
    2 cups sugar
    2 tsp soda
    ½ tsp salt
    1 cup sour milk
    1 cup oil
    2 tsp vanilla
    1 cup hot water

Mix all ingredients together. Bake in greased and floured 9x13 inch pan at 325° for 45 minutes. Cool and ice with the following.

Icing:
    2 cups sugar
    ½ cup cocoa

Combine above and gradually add:
½ cup milk

Add and stir constantly until boils:
½ cup butter
Boil 1½ minutes, then add ½ cup chopped nuts (optional)

Hamburger and Rice with Fried Bananas

—Gladys got this recipe from a British friend who served this dish when they lived in Nigeria.

Brown together:
    1 lb. hamburger
    ½ cup chopped onion
    Add 1½- cups water; thicken with cornstarch
    1 tsp garlic salt
    3 tbsp soy sauce

Slice several bananas or plantains the long way. Sauté in butter for a few minutes and remove from pan. Place hamburger mixture on top of cooked rice. Arrange bananas or plantains on top of the hamburger and serve.

Egusi Soup with Foo-Foo (Nigeria)
—Recipe from Nnenna Eni—Nnenna worked for the Grasse family in Abiriba, Nigeria and later moved to the United States with her husband and four children.

1 Chicken—Put the chicken in a large soup pot and cover with cold water. Heat to boil, and simmer until the chicken meat falls off of the bones. (May cut up in pieces).

For Soup:
- 2 packages frozen chopped spinach (10 oz) or 2 bags fresh spinach chopped (10 oz)
- 1 package frozen okra (10oz)—chop okra after thawed, or put in blender for few minutes
- 1 bag frozen (12 oz) or raw shrimp (10–15)—put shrimp in blender for few minutes
- 1 cup of chicken broth
- 1 cup ground Egusi *seeds
- Pinch of red pepper and salt to taste

Mix ingredients together and simmer for 10–15 minutes. Add chicken to soup mixture.

*Egusi seeds come from a melon grown in West Africa. Order Egusi ground seeds from Amazon.com or Afrofood.com

For Foo-Foo:
- 1½ cup water
- ½ cup Cream of Wheat

Mix together well and place in microwave for 1 minute. Remove from microwave and stir well, making sure there are no lumps. Place in microwave again for 1 minute.

Foo-foo is meant to be eaten with your fingers. Break off a piece of foo-foo and dip it into the soup. Traditional Foo-foo is made from pounded yam.

FAMILY FAVORITE Recipes

Oven Chicken Fricassee
—Grasse family Sunday dinner favorite.

2½–3 lb chicken cut in pieces, place skin side up in baking dish

Blend together and spread over chicken:
- 3 tbsp butter
- 3 tbsp flour
- 1 tsp salt
- 1 tsp poultry seasoning
- ½ tsp paprika
- Bake uncovered for 20 minutes at 375°.
- Mix together:
- 1 can cream of mushroom soup
- 6 oz. can or ⅔ cup evaporated milk
- ½ cup water

Pour over chicken and bake for 30 minutes more. Baste chicken 1–2 times while baking. Serve over hot rice.

Ice Cream Rice Krispy Dessert
—Gladys often prepared this dessert to serve to "spur of the moment" guests. She was prepared to invite church guests home for Sunday lunch.

Mix together and toast in 300 degree oven for 30 min in shallow baking pan:
- 2½ cup rice cereal
- 1 cup flake coconut
- 1 cup pecan pieces
- ½ cup butter, melted
- Add after above is toasted but while still warm:
- 3/4 cup brown sugar

Stir to blend.

Put ½ of mixture in bottom of 9"x13" pan. Cut vanilla ice cream to cover 1 inch thick. Sprinkle on remaining mixture and freeze. Cut in squares to serve.

Recipes, Food and Cooking— Family Memories

- Dad's smoked ham that he cured from pigs he raised and butchered himself.
- Vegetables that came out of our garden, fresh, canned, or frozen.
- Dad's apple tree orchard. We made apple cider and applesauce.
- Mom's ham, green beans, and red potatoes recipe, all from the backyard garden.
- Homemade sauerkraut in a crock.
- Homemade pretzels and root beer.
- Ice cream with salty pretzels.

—contributed by Carol Grasse

Wild game included more common things such as venison, squirrel, trout, as well as river eel, raccoon, frog legs, and snapping turtle—hunted and fished by local residents. Nothing was wasted, such as hunters killing raccoon for the pelt and tossing the meat, or fishermen discarding trout after enjoyment of fishing was over. They learned that Doc Grasse would take whatever they did not want.

—contributed by Chloe Grasse

Mom got a lot of recipes from *Grit* magazine, a weekly newspaper popular in rural America during much of the 20th century. It was sold door-to-door by local residents.

- Egg and sausage casserole for breakfast
- Spaghetti and meatballs
- Fried tomatoes on toast
- Sweet potatoes with tomato gravy
- Broccoli and raisin salad
- Oyster stuffing
- Baked squash (Granma Landis' recipe)
- Baked beans on toast for breakfast (we ate this in British guesthouses and on our trip through England returning from Africa)
- Dad's caramel popcorn (mix it in a brown paper sack or it doesn't taste right)
- Homemade butter pecan ice cream (Dad roasted the pecans in a cast iron skillet with butter)
- Sour cream raisin pie (Mennonite Community Cookbook recipe)
- Scotch shortbread cookies (from Nigeria)

—contributed by Mark Grasse

Gallery

Gladys' Forebears & Family

Gladys' great grandmother Catharine Freed Stover Rickert, her mother's father's mother.

Gladys' great grandmother Maria Moyer Hunsicker Baum, her mother's mother's mother.

With Faith and Persistence

Stover's Mill, Blooming Glen, Pennsylvania circa 1900.

Galdys' mother, Mamie Landis, standing by her coleus beds. She overwintered coleus cuttings in the enclosed porch on the right.

Gladys' father, Ephraim Landis, as a young man.

Gallery

Uncle Ervin Moyer in the first Buick he purchased. Circa 1915.

Ephraim and Mamie Landis relaxing at home. Note the door behind them decorated with Christmas card greetings.

Gladys' father, Ephraim Landis, doing a painting project in the backyard.

111

Ephraim and Mamie Landis, 1954.

Left to right, back row: Ephraim Landis, Walton Angstadt, Alvin Landis; middle row: Stella Schmell, Mamie Landis, Annie Angstadt, Lizzie Kulp, Katie Long, Nora Landis, Alice Landis; Front row: Stella Mae Schmell, Stella Landis. (Note that there were two Stella Schmells in the family.)

Gallery

Arkansas Communities

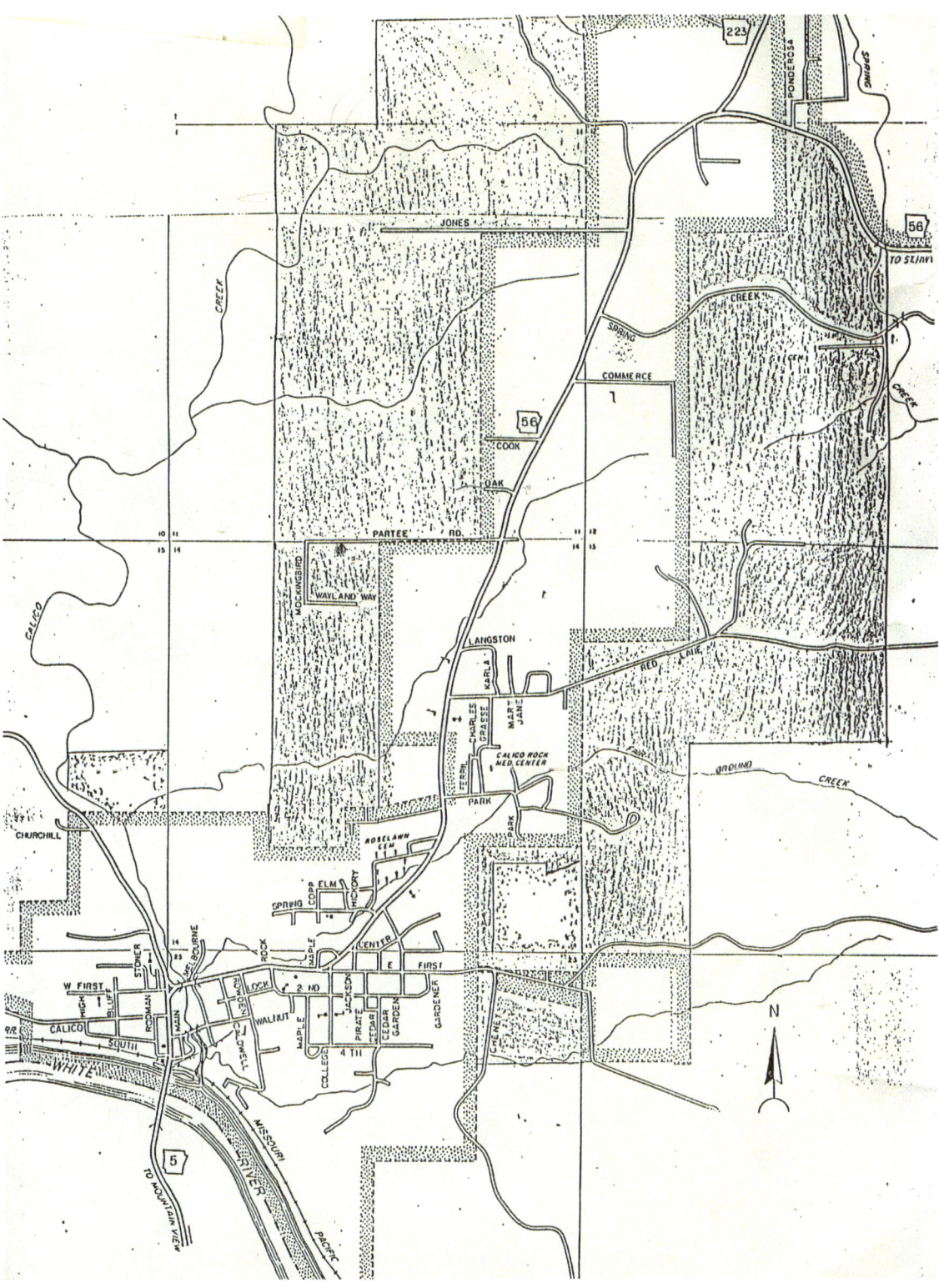

Map of Calico Rock, Arkansas, 1970s.

Pineville, Arkansas, about 3.5 miles from Calico Rock, in the 1950s around the time when the Grasses moved to Arkansas.

Right: A view from Calico Rock, Arkansas, 2014.

Community Medical Center of Izard County, Calico Rock, Arkansas, 2005.

Gallery

Left: Frank Horst was pastor of the Bethel Springs Mennonite Church at Culp for a time. According to Gladys, "He was a good minister and did a great job interacting with the local people. He and his wife LaVerne and their six girls and one boy served the community for a number of years. He came back to visit the area when he was 90 years old, and 70 people came out to a potluck to greet him."

Above: Newspaper clipping showing the then-new Grasse home-clinic built in Calico Rock in 1957.

Gladys, Meryl, and Mary Margaret Grasse along with hospital staff.

With Faith and Persistence

Meryl's Forebears and Family

Above: Meryl's great-grandparents Christian and Amanda Hockman and their family. Left to right: Christian, Harvey, Amanda holding William, Ida (who married David A. Detweiler, became mother of Sam and Wilma), and Bertha (who married John M. Landis, became mother of Lillian Landis Grasse.)

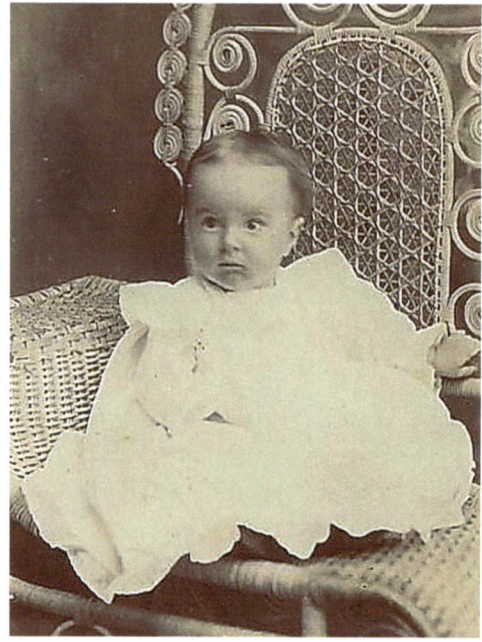

Merly's mother, Lillian Hockman Landis, as a child. She was born July 6, 1900.

Gallery

Left to right: Meryl's maternal grandparents John M. Landis and Bertha Landis, Eva Landis, and her husband, Samuel Landis (brother to John), vacationing. From back of picture: "Daytona Beach, Fla. Drove 15 miles on beach, Feb 1933. Reach Jacksonville, Fla. 7 o'clock pm Feb 18. Start at Lansdale Feb 16 7 o'clock am." (Photo courtesy of Eva Beidler)

Left to right: Samuel Landis, Eva Landis, Bertha Landis, John M. Landis, in Florida, 1933. (Photo courtesy of Eva Beidler)

John L. Grasse, Meryl's brother. John's efforts were important to the success of the Grasse medical work in Arkansas.

Above, Left to right: Nancy Grasse, John L. Grasse, Peggy Grasse, Mary Margaret Grasse, Philip Grasse.

Left: John L. Grasse and Mary Margaret Grasse.

Other Photos

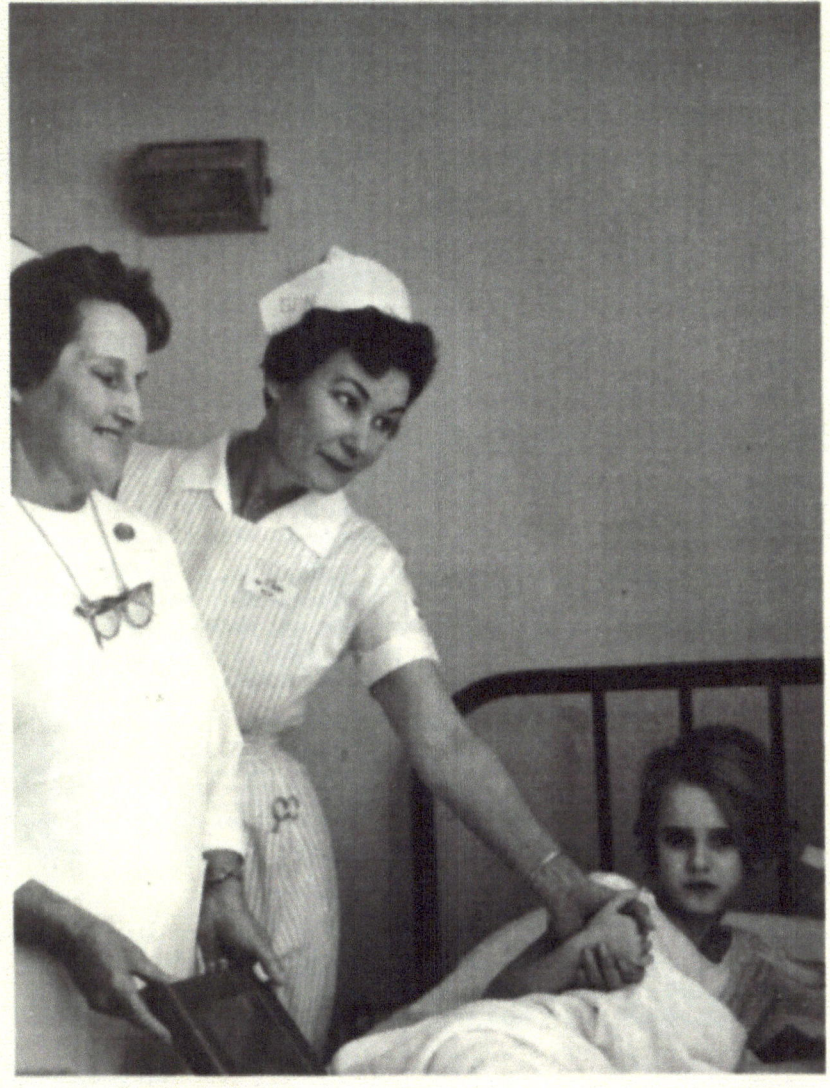

The ministry in Calico Rock was featured on the cover of The Christian Nurse for May–June 1969, a publication of the Mennonite Board of Missions. Left to right: "Mrs. Fulbright (LPN teacher), LPN Student, little girl Paine who had severely burned legs."

With Faith and Persistence

Above: Home Health and Hospice offering of Community Medical Center of Izard County (located across from the hospital.)

Left: Meryl Grasse fills balloons at the Community Medical Center of Izard County's 40th anniversary celebration, 1999.

Below: Heliport at Community Medical Center of Izard County.

Gallery

April 2007 dedication of hospital addition that included two operating room suites, a new emergency room, central supply, recovery room, new hospital waiting room, and surgical nurses' stations, chapel, and enlarged physical therapy space.

Gladys in the kitchen of the Grasse home on Highway 56, Calico Rock.

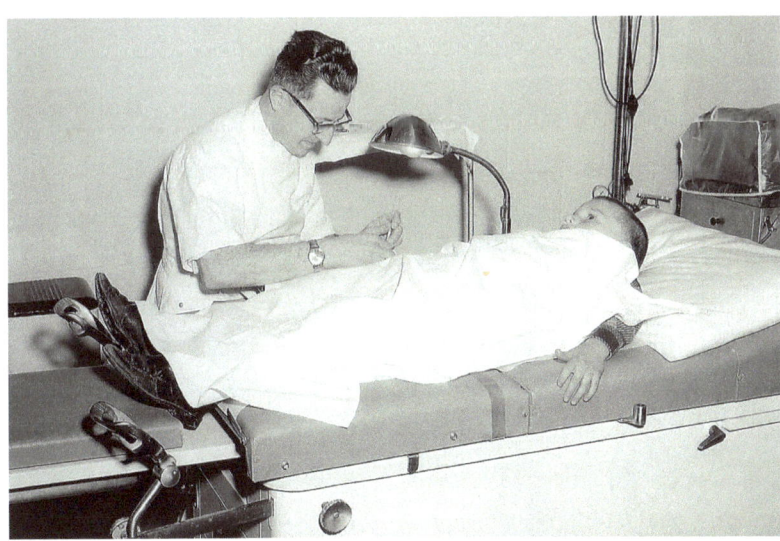

Meryl Grasse attending to a patient.

Meryl Grasse and a hospital vehicle.

During 50-year celebration of opening of the first hospital, 2009, on the porch of "The Little White House," left to right: Angela Richmond, CEO, Meryl Grasse, Mary Margaret Grasse, Gladys Grasse.

Gallery

Newspaper article in White River Current *highlighting Grasse family plans to go to Nigeria, 1964.*

Below: Left to right: Carol Grasse, Karen Grasse, Chloe Grasse, Meryl Grasse, Nnenna Eni, Gladys Grasse, Mark Grasse, Joel Grasse, Gwendolyn Grasse, 2012.

Grasse family gathers to celebrate Gladys and Meryl's 60th wedding anniversary, Ciao Restaurant, Little Rock, Arkansas, 2012.

Gladys and Meryl Grasse with flowers honoring their 60th wedding anniversary.

Relaxing at home, 336 Red Lane, Calico Rock, Arkansas, with granddaughter. Left to right: Gladys Grasse, Meryl Grasse, Elleanna.

Nnenna Eni, Meryl Grasse, Gladys Grasse by the White River, Calico Rock, Arkansas.

With Faith and Persistence

Four generations. Left to right: Joseph, Jayden, Joel, A. Meryl.

Gladys and Meryl, 1997

Genealogy

Gladys' Forebears

Reuben Rosenberger Landis
October 12, 1864–October 19, 1951

Ephraim Moyer Landis
September 29, 1900–May 16, 1981

Lizzie Metz Moyer Landis
March 9, 1865–August 9, 1940

Gladys Stover
Landis Grasse
January 17, 1926

Edwin Freed Stover
December 6, 1869–May 2, 1928

Mamie Baum Stover Landis
June 18, 1902–December 16, 1987

Ida Hunsicker Baum Stover
March 26, 1873–November 22, 1920

Meryl's Forebears

Oliver Henry Grass
July 31, 1865–January 12, 1960

Anthony Meyers Grasse
June 18, 1892–April 25, 1982

Hannah R. Meyers Grass
March 9, 1868–November 10, 1942

Anthony Meryl Grasse
May 16, 1923–
January 29, 2016

John Moyer Landis
September 25, 1876–February 4, 1949

Lillian Hockman Landis Grasse
July 6, 1900–September 5, 1988

Bertha Kulp Hockman Landis
August 16, 1879–September 5, 1965

Gladys & Meryl Descendants
Children, Grandchildren, and Great-grandchildren

Anthony Meryl Grasse and Gladys S. Landis Grasse married

Children:

Karen
Joel
Mark
Chloe
Carol
Gwendolyn

    Joel married Susan
- Joseph
- Joshua

        Joseph married Angela
- Jayden
- Olivia

    Chloe married Linford
- Hannah
- Mariah

        Hannah married Clay

        Mariah married Jonathan

    Carol married Daniel (deceased)
Engaged to Abraham (Abe)

    Gwendolyn married Steve
- Elleanna

Thanks to Jean Kilheffer Hess, oral historian and life story book project manager, of StoryShare, LLC, who worked alongside our daughter Karen to bring this book into being.

www.ingramcontent.com/pod-product-compliance
Lightning Source LLC
Chambersburg PA
CBHW041411160426

42811CB00106B/1634